41 SPECIAL WALKS

IN

SOUTHERN ANDALUCIA

PATRICK ELVIN

LIST OF WALKS

WALK 102	MARBELLA - LA CONCHA FROM ISTAN	25
WALK 103	TORRECILLA FROM QUEJIGALES	29
WALK 104	RONDA - UP THE HIDALGA	33
WALK 105	RONDA - UP THE ALMOLA	37
WALK 106	RONDA - CUEVA DEL GATO	40
WALK 107	RONDA - TAJO ABANICO	44
WALK 108	RONDA - CERRO ALCOJADA	49
WALK 109	CARTAJIMA - PUJERRA AND JUZCAR	53
WALK 110	MONTEJAQUE - VENTANA	57
WALK 111	MONTEJAQUE - CERRO DE MONTALITE	63
WALK 112	MONTEJAQUE - LLANO DE LIBAR	67
WALK 113	CORTES – THE SCULPTURES WALK	72
WALK 114	CORTES - GARGANTA LAS PULGAS	82

WALK 115 ATAJATE TO JIMERA DE LIBAR RETURN VIA LOMO DE LAS MORILLAS 85

WALK 116 BENADALID TO ATAJATE 89

WALK 117 BENADALID - EL DORSAL 92

WALK 118 ALGATOCIN - VENTA SAN JUAN TO BENARRABA VIA TRAIL DE BICI - RETURN VIA LLANOS DEL REY 95

WALK 119 ALGATOCIN TO VENTA SAN JUAN – RETURN VIA GR 249 AND LLANOS DEL REY 100

WALK 120 ALGATOCIN – TOWARDS BENARRABA - RETURN VIA LOS GUINDALES, INSTITUTO AND LAS PILAS 103

WALK 121 JUBRIQUE – VENTA S. JUAN TO JUBRIQUE 107

WALK 122 GENALGUACIL ON GR249 RETURN VIA BAÑOS DE DUQUE 110

WALK 123 CASARES – CRESTELLINA	113
WALK 124 CASARES – RIO MANILVA	118
WALK 125 CASARES TO LACIPO	122
WALK 126 GRAZALEMA - CERRO DE LOS COROS	125
WALK 127 GRAZALEMA - CAMPOBUCHE	129
WALK 128 GRAZALEMA - RELOJ/SIMANCON	132
WALK 129 GRAZALEMA - PINSAPAR	135
WALK 130 GRAZALEMA - TORREON AND THE GARGANTA VERDE (2 WALKS IN ONE DAY)	139
WALK 131 BENAOCAZ TO JAULETAS	141
WALK 132 VILLALUENGA - RELOJ/SIMANCON	144
WALK 133 JIMENA – VULTURES, ROCK POOLS AND ROCK SLABS	147
WALK 134 CASTELLAR - CASTILLO TO THE CUEVA DE LOS MAQUIS	151
WALK 135 CASTELLAR - SENDERO MARAPOSA	154
WALK 136 CASTELLAR - EMBALSE GUADARRANQUE	158
WALK 137 CASTELLAR - TORRETA DEL MORO	161
WALK 138 CASTELLAR TO THE PINAR DEL REY	164
WALK 139 GIBRALTAR - MEDITERRANEAN STEPS	167
WALK 140 LOS BARRIOS - BACINETE	172
WALK 141 ALGECIRAS - ARROYO DEL MIEL	176
WALK 142 ALGECIRAS- PUERTO DEL VIENTO - GARGANTA DEL CAPITAN	180

RONDA AREA – WALKS 103 - 108

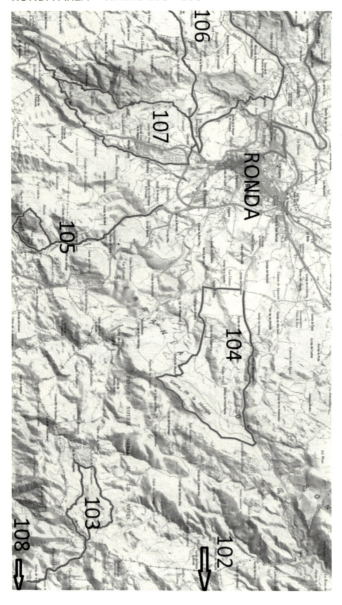

CORTES DE LA FRONTERA – WALKS 113 – 114

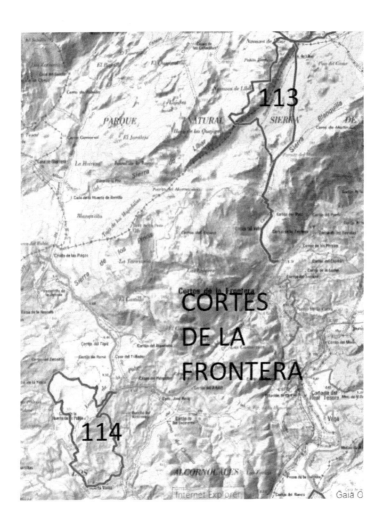

WEST AND SOUTH OF RONDA – WALKS 110-112 AND 115-117

ALGATOCIN AND BENARRABA WALKS 118 - 122

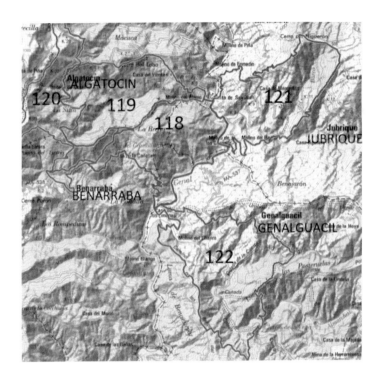

CASARES WALKS 123- 125

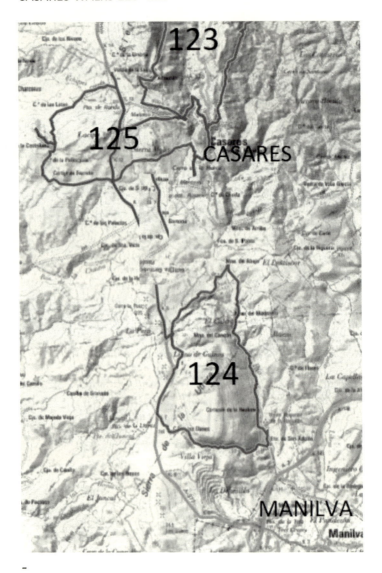

GRAZALEMA AND VILLALENGUA WALKS 126 – 132

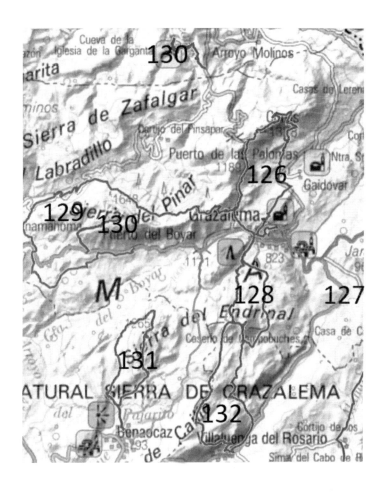

CASTELLAR   WALKS 134 - 138

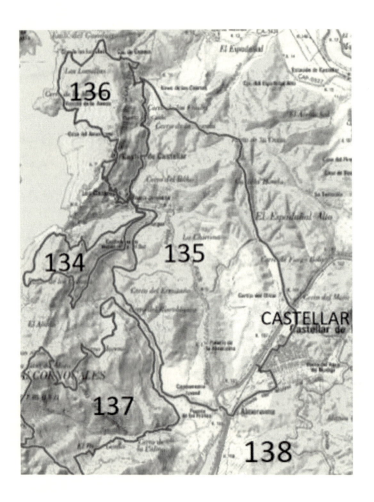

WALKS 139 AND 141 – 142

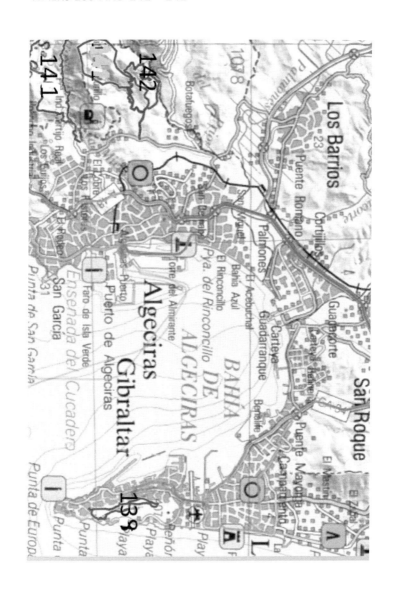

THE AUTHOR

I first came to this area in 1976 to visit my parents and since then had a hankering to live here. The chance came in 1997 when I was able to move to a country *finca* (smallholding) along with my wife. I soon began to explore the local area and acquired an extensive knowledge of the footpath system throughout the whole of the Serrania de Ronda and further afield, also working as a walking guide and running a walking club for friends and visitors.

These walks are the result of a demand for full-day walks and the setting up of a weekly full-day walk, based on Gaucin but which has extended to a radius of 60 kilometres up and down the A369 and A 405 respectively to include Ronda and Grazalema at one end and Algeciras and Tarifa to the south. Marbella and Casares to the east have great walks in this book.

I am indebted to colleagues from the walking club for proof testing the written instructions for the walks, thus enabling local residents and visitors to enjoy this great walking area with the added insurance that the routes have been tested independently.

This book is a companion to my first three publications "50 Walks Around Gaucin", "40 Half day walks in the Serrania de Ronda and Jimena area" and 40 day walks in Southern Andalucía also published by AMAZON.

THE AREA

All the walks are in the provinces of Malaga and Cadiz, the two provinces that comprise the most southerly point of Spain. There is also one spectacular walk in Gibraltar, well worth crossing the border for.

MALAGA   This province is probably best known for the Costa del Sol, a popular holiday destination. You only have to drive 10 minutes into the impressive looking hills that flank the coast and a whole new world opens up, especially for walkers. Inland from Marbella is the ancient town of Ronda perched on the Tajo gorge, surrounded by the Parque Natural de la Sierra de las Nieves, with the 1916 metre high Torrecilla. Walk 103 climbs this impressive peak with views inland and down to the coast. There are five walks based on Ronda. Further inland from Ronda there are more mountain ranges including the Sierra de Libar behind the village of Cortes de la Frontera. South of Ronda are two fine river valleys, the Guadiaro and the Genal and there are several walks based here. This area is known as the Serrania de Ronda and one of its principal villages is Gaucin, a popular holiday destination for the discerning traveller as well as the home of the author. I have published a separate book of walks around Gaucin available from Amazon.

Nearer the coast is the village of Casares where there are two fine walks, and I have included one walk near Marbella up the impressive peak of La Concha by means of a little known but spectacular route.

CADIZ

This province is the most southerly of Spain and includes both the Mediterranean and Atlantic coasts, the latter known as the Costa de la Luz. The coast near Tarifa is noted for its sandy beaches and for its winds.

Inland, the Alcornocales Natural Park is the largest area of cork oak habitat on the Iberian peninsular. Several walks including those round Jimena, Castellar and Alcala are based on the Park. Further north there is the smaller but spectacular Grazalema Natural Park which includes the highest peak in the province, the Torreon. This mountain range enjoys the highest rainfall in Spain being the first point of contact for the prevailing westerlies bringing moisture in from the Atlantic, a factor to be borne in mind when out walking.

In summary this diverse terrain means this book contains a varied portfolio of walks, from mountain walks, walks in rolling hills, coastal walks and river walks, all in wonderful scenery.

THE BOOK AND HOW TO USE IT

The book is a no-frills practical guide to 51 diverse walks in the provinces of Malaga and Cadiz. It contains for each walk, brief statistics and description, how to get there, with a wikilocs map with recorded track enhanced to show up in black and white in the book with waymarks numbered to coincide with the text. I have converted the usual google earth background of wikilocs to a Raster map

1:10000 published by the Insituto Geografico Nacional (IGN), which shows a relief map with good mapping of paths and tracks, though I will stress that Spanish mapping is poor in relation to the British Ordnance Survey and shows many inconsistencies. You can access the 1:10000 raster maps by going onto http://signa.ign.es/signa/.

There are tutorials on how to download the maps free of charge on YouTube: https://www.youtube.com/watch?v=nU2DOX0d8fg&t=47s

I have added the wikiloc link to each walk just below each map. These are downloadable free of charge to your device from wikilocs, but to follow the track on your device on the walk itself you will need to subscribe to Wikiloc. At the time of writing it is about 8 euros a year, and well worth this nominal sum.

Here is a brief summary of how to use wikiloc.

1. Press explore. (you do not have to be on internet to navigate as the system uses GPS but it is essential to download and save the wikiloc track while you are on the internet if you don't have 3G or 4G on your smart phone)

2. under search text or wikiloc ID enter the unique track number

3. the track will show on the page on google maps or google earth background (to change map background press the world map icon)

4. Press the photo. (subscribe at this point if not already done, it's about 8 euros a year)

5. Press follow trail

6. A blue dot will appear which is your position. Adjust your position on the ground to maintain the dot on the track. If you are some distance from the start you will be asked if you want directions. If so you will be redirected to google maps which will give you driving directions. When you reach the start you can switch over to the wikilocs track.

7. Small yellow markers show photo/waypoints. Press on one to see photo and accompanying instruction. With the latest version you will get a notification bell indicating you are close to a waypoint and a written instruction or piece of information will appear at the top of your screen.

8. If you stray off the route a sort of low squealy sound will come from your device, when you regain the track a more bell like noise will sound.

9. At the end of the walk, you can save your own track locally which has been created during the walk; to enter it into the public domain you will need internet coverage.

I hasten to add that it is not a prerequisite to do these walks with wikiloc, it is only there as a back up to the text. If, like me, you prefer a text with a hard copy map then you will manage very well without wikiloc. But I will specify in the walk description if a particular route will be a lot easier if you use the wikiloc track especially if there is no path to follow.

TERMINOLOGY   The English language has a wonderfully diverse vocabulary and is a global influence, but I am conscious that this global diversity produces complications within the walking fraternity, so I will endeavour to explain what I mean when I use certain walking terminology.

Path: this is short for footpath and describes a route which is only passable on foot and can range in standard from a goat path to a paved path of a metre or so in width. I use narrow and wide to specify the width, narrow being only wide enough for one person.

Track: in this book it means a route that is wide enough for a four-wheeled vehicle to use. Its surface can be as basic as earth or it can be concreted or even tarmacked. It applies to all vehicular routes which are not assigned a road number by the authorities. There is an enormous network of tracks, but in some cases the local authorities are beginning to adopt them for maintenance purposes as more and more vehicles are in evidence in rural Spain.

Trail: only refers to a route in general, not used to describe a type of path or track. A term used by wikiloc and americans to describe a path but not used in this context in this book.

RIGHTS OF WAY

As in most countries there is an issue as to whether some public rights of way exist or whether the landowner can prohibit access. This area is no exception, and perhaps is a prime example in Spain where there is poor or non-existent documentation on ownership and rights of way, so there are several grey areas. In the past this has not mattered, but in this age of increased mobility, leisure time and access to the countryside, combined with more proprietorial owners, some rights of way have become contentious. In this area there are theoretically undisputed historical public rights of way, known as cañadas (up to 75 metres wide) and veredas (15 metres wide): an example in this book is the Vereda del Pescadero (walk 124). These were drovers' routes.

Another category is the Via Pecuaria, another form of agricultural right of way, which is recorded very inaccurately on documents held in town halls called 'Croquis de las Vias Pecuarias del Termino Municipal de ………' For example, Gaucin`s dates from 1968.

Another important feature is the publicly owned land around Gaucin and Jimena known as Monte Publico. Examples include the lower slopes of the Hacho mountain and the forested land north of the village to the west of the main Ronda road. This land is freely accessible to the public. The only drawback is that on very rare occasions the area could be closed off as a fire risk or for tree-felling or other work.

Signposted walks

In the past 20 years Spain at local and national level has introduced the European system of path marking. This consists of:

1: red and white markers for long distance paths (Gran recorridos) (GR). Examples found here are the GR 141 Gran Senda de la Serranía de Ronda, the GR 249 Gran Senda de Malaga , and the GR 7 Tarifa to Athens path.

2: Yellow and white markers for medum distance paths (pequenos recorridos) (PR), generally linking villages. You will see these frequently on these walks.

3: Green and white markers for local paths (senda local) (SL). Created and marked up by town halls, these are paths that start and finish in a particular village.

Lastly there are local paths, not necessarily recorded in public documents, or marked, which villagers have used for centuries to reach their *fincas* (smallholdings), and which pass through other people's land. These are probably the most contentious; many are regarded by the authorities as public rights of way for agricultural workers, but in recent times they have begun to be used for leisure activities like walking and riding, and at the same time the owners of the land they pass through, often new owners not previously connected with the countryside are demanding, and attempting to enforce, their privacy. A mystery person has marked up several paths around Gaucin with blue paint which is generally very useful but these are not guaranteed rights of way.

However, there are some local paths that are definitely public and these can be found in the 1968 document mentioned above and the equivalents in all the villages in this area held by the local town halls.

Notwithstanding all of the above, in nearly 40 years of walking in this area I have only been challenged as a potential trespasser on about 4 occasions, and on none of the routes in this book.

I have enjoyed several long discussions with the *enginero forestal* (land surveyor) of Gaucin town hall, David Garcia, about rights of way and I am grateful to him for his advice.

GENERAL INFORMATION ABOUT WALKING

The best time of year to visit the area is in Spring and Autumn when the climate is most suitable for walking; however the winters can be warm with good visibility – you just need to be aware of the rains that can come between November and April and the heat that is ever present in July and August. It is possible to walk all year round – it is just necessary to choose the appropriate time of day according to the season.

In this area trees include cork oaks, Holm oaks, chestnuts, pines, poplars, carobs, almonds, olives and figs. Due to the predominance of evergreen species, even in winter the impression is always one of abundant greenery.

Within the woodland is abundant undergrowth, with gorse, broom, heathers and lavender, and of course many perennial wild flowers, such as the narcissus in winter and the orchids and peonies in spring. The quieter walker may be lucky and see fox, mongoose, badger and wild boar - the latter evident through its excavating activities. Birdlife is ever present and ranges from the Griffon vultures and other raptors to the numerous migratory birds which pass through the Genal and Guadiaro valleys in March and

September. Cattle, sheep, pigs and goats are prevalent in the area; if you are lucky you may see the Ibex Iberico, a cross between a deer and goat which is common in the mountains around. Deer are also found in the area.

Of course, the main attraction of walking in this area is the opportunity to enjoy the marvellous views in all directions. On the southern horizon, beyond the hills between the Valleys of the Genal and the Guadiaro Rivers, looms the Rock of Gibraltar with the Rif mountains of Africa behind it. To the East lies the wooded valley of the Genal, with its scattered white villages framed by the red- rocked Sierra Bermeja and the rugged peaks of the Crestellina range. To the north are the bare peaks of the Sierra de las Nieves, and to the west, from the top of the Hacho mountain, one can see the valley of the Guadiaro with open fields and La Buitrera, a deep limestone gorge eroded by the river Guadiaro and inhabited by the eponymous vulture with the Sierra de Libar behind the village of Cortes. At the southern end the valley of the Hozgarganta behind Jimena forms one of the boundaries of the Natural Park of the Alcornocales, one of the largest wild areas of Europe.

Finally, I offer the usual but vital advice. I am sure that all walking enthusiasts will be aware that the weather can change rapidly in this part of Spain on the border between the Mediterranean and Atlantic climates. Make sure you allow enough daylight for your walk. Take something to drink and, for the longer walks, something to eat. It is imperative to have comfortable footwear with well-gripping soles, and advisable to wear long trousers as the paths are sometimes a little overgrown and gorse is prevalent.

In the warmer seasons sun cream and/or a hat is recommended. Please respect the environment, remember to close all gates which you have had to open. Do not disturb the farm animals you may come across especially if you are accompanied by dogs; these must always be on a lead.

Please be aware that new gates and fences may appear which do not feature in the descriptions: I would be most grateful to hear about these, and also to receive any comments and suggested alterations in English or Spanish for future editions of this guide book: please send to the email address below: robertpatrickelvin@gmail.com

MORE INFORMATION ABOUT WALKING IN GAUCIN AND OTHER ACTIVITIES

Gaucín Walking club. The author organises walks in the area free of charge, on two week-days every week from September to June, ranging from 2 to 7 hours. You can contact him for further details: robertpatrickelvin@gmail.com or go to Facebook and enter Gaucin walkers in the group section if you wish to join in.

Any updates on walks, such as fallen trees or overgrown paths, in all the walk books will also be posted in the Gaucin walkers page

MORE BOOKS ON WALKING

Patrick Elvin's Amazon publications cover the following areas in Andalucia.

Southern Andalucia: 40 day walks in southern Andalucia between Ronda and Jimena.

Serrania de Ronda: 40 half day walks in the Serrania de Ronda and the Jimena area.

Walks around Gaucin contains 50 walks based on the village of Gaucin.

Jimena de la Frontera: 25 walks around Jimena de la Frontera.

La Alpujarra: 10 special walks in La Alpujarra

Aracena: 10 special walks in the Sierra de Aracena

Editorial La Serranía S.L., 2007 published Valle del Genal, Guia del Excursionísta by Rafael Floris Dominguez with 57 trails for walking and cycling, in Spanish.

ACKNOWLEDGEMENTS

My wife Susan who has tirelessly edited every page with her indomitable thoroughness.

WALK 102 - LA CONCHA CIRCULAR FROM ISTAN NEAR MARBELLA

Time: 7 - 8 hours (17 kilometres)

Difficulty: hard

Terrain: mainly very rough paths; some rock scrambling

BRIEF DESCRIPTION: one of the best walks in the area much preferable to the very popular route from the refugio above Ojen. It is a challenging route with some rock scrambling on the ascent, and a path sometimes hard to follow but the views from the top are worth the effort.

HOW TO GET THERE: Take the only road to Istan from Puerto Banus. As you enter the village look for a steep road up to the right signposted Altos de Istan and after 100 metres turn right at a mini roundabout. Continue up the hill passing a sports complex (polideportivo). Park in the carpark on the right just beyond.

THE WALK: from the car park continue up the road keeping the Hotel Altos de Istan on your right. In front of you there are some finger posts indicating various walks. Take the one to the right PR135 to La Concha. It follows the contour line briefly before turning up a bank to the left and reducing to a rough stony path. This path will lead all the way to the Concha ridge. It is waymarked with yellow and white flashes interspersed with frequent cairns. Care will be needed as you cross over the three cols and the path is unpredictable at these points. At the first col (MAP 1) turn right at the waymark and the path drops down to the right of the ridge running up to your left. (The wikiloc track has a small offshoot here where the author went wrong)

MAP 1 THE FIRST AND LAST PART OF THE CONCHA WALK

https://www.wikiloc.com/wikiloc/view.do?id=21128532

alternative wikiloc track with error removed but no waypoint photographs

https://www.wikiloc.com/wikiloc/view.do?id=21137997

At the second col (MAP 2) the path climbs a little before entering the next valley and then dropping down to cross the gully below. There is some scrambling before arriving at the next col (MAP 3). From here you go straight up the ridge. You pass a waymark post, then the path becomes rather indistinct and you will have to rely on the

MAP 2 THE MIDDLE PART OF THE CONCHA WALK

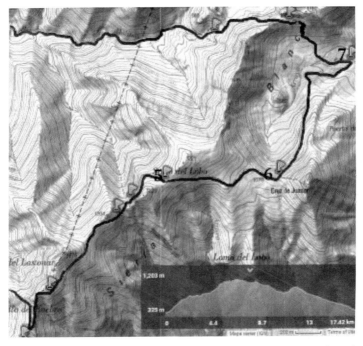

occasional cairn. When you are level with the ridge ahead which is the Concha ridge the path will level out and traverse along the contour line to reach this ridge.

At this point (MAP 4) it is possible to continue to the right out to the Concha peak. You should allow an extra hour. Return the same way and then follow the ridge to your left. This is a popular route so don't be surprised at the number of people on this section. The path passes to the right of a peak and where it is very precipitous, there are chains to help you keep your footing.

The path drops down to a saddle between two peaks, passes through, drops steeply then passes along the left side of the next peak. As it rises to the ridge to your right, just before the top, ignore a path to the left marked with large cairns. (MAP 5) Pass over the top and follow the path as it turns left to drop down gradually below the right side of the ridge. Ahead is the Cruz de Juanar a small hermitage atop the next peak. This can be another diversion, time and energy permitting. At the next junction marked by a finger post (MAP 6) turn left down into woods and follow this path for 20 minutes through pine trees.

At the next junction of paths, turn left where there is a signpost saying ISTAN 6 kilometres. You will enjoy a brief few moments of flat walking before you pass a small brick building and begin a zigzag climb up to the ridge in front of you. Cross over the ridge and start descending along the rough path, ignoring one turn to the right which drops down the hill.

Your path continues straight ahead through rocks, then descends into the valley ahead. At one point there is a good-looking path to the left which you should ignore, instead taking a less appetising path into scrubby bushes marked by cairns. This marks the start of a long descent along a stream bed in a narrow gully flanked by steep mountainside. You need to be a little vigilant here as from time to time the path leaves the stream bed to avoid overgrown sections, steep drops and to cut off corners. Yellow and white flashes and cairns will guide you at these points.

Eventually after passing through metal gates indicating Campo de Tiro (clay pigeon shooting area) the streambed encounters a dam wall and the path ascends steeply up to the left. You pass through the clay pigeon shooting shelter to join a driveable track which leads down to the car park.

WALK 103 RONDA- SIERRA DE LAS NIEVES- TORRECILLA

Time: 6.5 hours (17 kilometres)

Difficulty: hard due to climb

Terrain: rough mountain paths

BRIEF DESCRIPTION: a popular walk up Malaga province's second highest mountain, with a variant ascent to make a more interesting day than the standard up and down route. The views from the top encompass the coastline between Malaga and Gibraltar to the east and the Sierra de Grazalema to the west. On a clear day you can see the Sierra Nevada to the north east.

HOW TO GET THERE: take the Ronda to San Pedro road A376 and turn into the Parque Natural Sierra de las Nieves between K 137 and 136. Drive 10 kilometres to the Area Recreativa Las Quejigales, ignoring any turnoffs. Park here.

THE WALK: head north out of the car park on a track, (passing the panel board showing the standard route up Torrecilla on your right) (MAP 1), for almost exactly a kilometre passing a turn off to the left after 800 metres. You reach the Puerto de Quejigales (MAP 2). Take the right fork here. After 600 metres pass by the Fuente La Molina, where the track reduces to a path marked by blobs of blue paint and cairns, then a kilometre further on, you need to keep right here (MAP 3) on a path known as the Cañada la Cañalizo which climbs into woods in an easterly direction well marked by cairns. It enters a gully and climbs up the stream bed and just under 2 kilometres later and at a height of 1700 metres, keep left to pass a grassy hollow on your right. (MAP 4)

After 400 metres keep straight on as you pass another hollow to your right containing a circular wall, a former "snow well" (Pozo de Nieve) used to store snow to be used as ice(MAP 5). Keep left at the next junction where there is a finger post (MAP 6) and soon you are heading south on open terrain with various small peaks on either side. After 20 minutes the path drops down and heads towards the mass of the Torrecilla ahead and passes by a small shrine dedicated to the Virgen del Pilar where there is a spring and water trough (MAP 7). Cross the small saddle and take the path which zigzags up the side of the Torrecilla to the peak at 1919 metres (MAP 8).

Return to the shrine the same way and then follow the same path to the Puerto de los Pilones, passing MAP 7 and MAP 6 and then leaving the snow well to your right with its explanatory panel. The path meets a driveable track by a panel with a large photo of the terrain around the Torrecilla (MAP 9). Turn left and go downhill for 200 metres and turn right off the track by a finger post (MAP 10) onto a rocky path descending into the woods. 700 metres from the start of the path, make sure you keep left where the path splits keeping within the wooded gully. You will pass down through wonderful woods containing the rare Pinsapo pine. From now on, the path should be easy to follow and you will see the car park and the refugio below. At the bottom turn left onto the track to rejoin your car.

31

MAP FOR FIRST AND LAST PART OF WALK

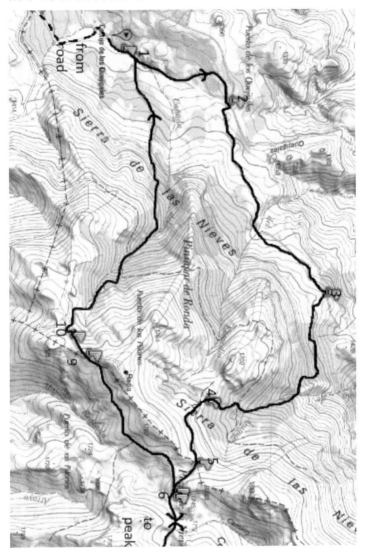

MAP FOR MIDDLE PART OF WALK

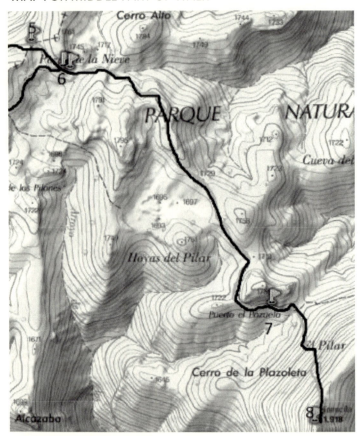

https://www.wikiloc.com/hiking-trails/walk-103-from-walk-book-special-walks-in-southern-andalucia-torrecilla-35697137

WALK 104 - RONDA - LA HIDALGA

Time: 6 hours (18 kilometres)

Difficulty: Hard due to climb

Terrain: track and cross country, rock scrambling

BRIEF DESCRIPTION: A rugged walk involving a climb up Ronda´s closest mountain La Hidalga at 1500 metres. Some of the walk is across open terrain. The first part of the route uses the GR 249 Ronda to El Burgo.

HOW TO GET THERE: take the ring road round Ronda direction Sevilla and at the one-way system at the north end take the first exit marked El Burgo. Turn immediately right into the Recinto Ferial where there are usually tourist coaches parked. Take a road heading to the left which is also the GR 243/249 marked with red and white flashes, past the entrance to a builders´ merchants and it will drop into a shallow valley and up the other side into countryside. Go for 3 kilometres until you reach a cross-roads of tracks with a house on the left just beforehand. Park here.

THE WALK: keep in the same direction heading east up the hill on the GR 243/249 marked with red and white flashes. You pass over a cattle grid after just over 2 kilometres (MAP 1) and after a further 4 kilometres, ignoring all side turnings, cross over another cattle grid which is enclosed in a gate. (MAP 2)

https://es.wikiloc.com/rutas-senderismo/ronda-hidalga-walk-103-from-book-special-walks-in-southern-andalucia-33058820

MAP FOR WALK 104

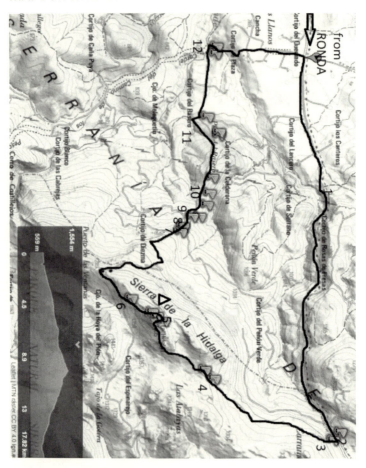

Immediately after the cattle grid turn right off the track, climb over the low wire fence and head up through bushes into an open area with a fence on your right. Head up hill and as the fence turns right, (MAP 3) follow the rough path alongside the fence for a few metres then leave the fence at 45 degrees as the rough path climbs up through a rocky area, marked by the occasional cairn. Keeping the fence to your right, edge right to start walking into a large rock-strewn plateau, heading due south. Sheep have made paths which make the route easier. Cross a shallow gully and 2 kilometres from MAP 3 pass through a wire fence by means of a wire and post gate (MAP 4).

Now the Hidalga mountain is looming up in front of you. Be careful as the main peak is behind the first peak you can see. So keep a little left as you start climbing and even when you have passed by the first summit, still keep to the left, and you will find the way up considerably easier. As in most mountain ascents without an actual footpath, there is no defined route so just find the best way you can. The wikilocs track as is good as any but the aim is to reach the trig point defined by a concrete pillar and is best approached from the south (MAP 5). From the top, head southwest and there will be a gravel track below, easily visible. Occasional cairns will show a good way down to the track (MAP 6).

Turn right and follow the track as it passes to the left of the radio masts ahead, then veers right and down the mountain side, now heading north. 2 kilometres from the radio masts, after a few zigzags, the track crosses a ridge and veers sharp left. At this point (MAP 7) leave the track, heading right, down the ridge; a cairn will indicate a rough path which runs downhill slightly to the left of the spine of the ridge through some scattered trees; there are frequent cairns to guide you.

At the bottom you should reach a track, the other side of which there is a metal water trough. (MAP 8) Cross over the track, leave the trough to your left and turn 30 degrees to your right down through the trees following cairns to another track about 100 metres below.

Turn left and soon arrive at fencing and some gates (MAP 9). Go through the gate facing you and veer right along a grassy track, running about 50 metres to the left and parallel to a fence on your right, towards a pylon. (The wikiloc track keeps to the right of the fence and then passes through the next gate on the left to join the grassy track) When the grassy track splits, (MAP 10) keep right and as this track approaches a gate in the fence, veer left off the track and take a small path through bushes keeping the fence to your right.

700 metres (10 minutes) after leaving the grassy track pass a gate in the fence and continue down to the bottom. (The wikilocs track goes through the gate, then through another gate just opposite and joins a rough track leading down to a gate which may be padlocked) The fence turns left, just go a further 50 metres down the slope and there is a gate. (MAP 11) Pass through and turn right up a good track which leads up the hill then turns left by a gate on the right.

Pass a grand entrance to a country property and continue down the hill. Near the bottom there is a bathing spot at a damned-up stream which could be refreshing if you are walking in warm weather. Otherwise keep going until you reach a junction (MAP 12). Turn right here by a sign Puerta Verde Ronda to Marbella. This track climbs out of the valley and leads you back to your car at the crossroads 1 kilometre further on.

WALK 105 RONDA – UP THE ALMOLA MOUNTAIN

Time: 6 hours (14.5 kilometres)

Difficulty: hard

Terrain: well-made path and rocky cross country: 10 minutes of rock scrambling.

BRIEF DESCRIPTION: a tough walk up a spectacular mountain overlooking Ronda. It begins and ends along a beautiful path recently restored by the Department of the Environment. Then there is a tough climb onto the high plateau of the Almola mountain, where you are rewarded with wonderful views. A reasonable descent takes you to a good track to rejoin your original path.

HOW TO GET THERE: Head out of Ronda on the A397 direction San Pedro and just past the new hospital on your right, take a wide track to the right opposite Venta La Higuera. Go 400 metres and park at this junction.

THE WALK: turn left at the junction and follow the track passing a few villas and drop into a valley. When you reach a fork in the track, (MAP 1) go left up the slope into woods. This rough track reduces to a path and follows a valley passing through a couple of gates. It is a well-made path lined with stones and rocks. It eventually crosses a stream bed, passes through a gate, then veers right past a spring and water trough. (MAP 2)

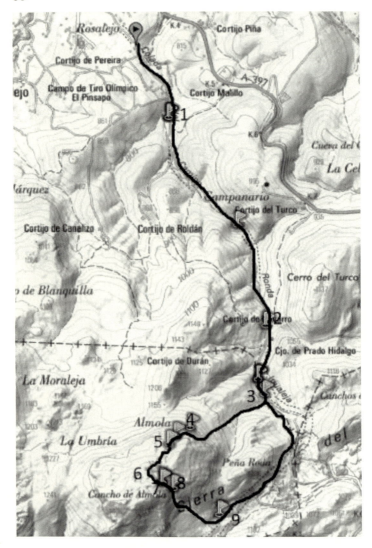

https://www.wikiloc.com/hiking-trails/walk-book-special-walks-in-southern-andalucia-almola-from-ronda-36189336

Just after the next gate and when you have crossed the streambed, look for a cairn marking the start of a very rough, barely visible path up a wide gully (MAP 3). Turn right and follow the right-hand side of the gully. There is no real path, so you need to head up the steep slope towards the cliffs of the Almola. The direction is south west. As you approach the base of the cliffs be aware of, and head for a ledge running left to right and up through a gap in the cliffs. You may need to scramble over some rocks and then reach a brown stained cleft in the rock face used by sheep and goats to access the upper part of the mountain (MAP 4). The direction is now west. Once up this cleft, the cliffs open up into a wide grassy gully/bowl. Head up the gully, climb the rocks at the end and then reach a grassy hollow. (MAP 5)

At this point, look ahead and there is a peak in front of you. Cross the hollow and clamber over rocks to the top of the ridge at 1387 metres. Just below, a long grassy gully runs at right angles to the direction you have been travelling (MAP 6). Drop down to the gully, turn left and follow this flat swathe south east until it reaches the edge of the large plateau and dramatically drops down the slope below with the small village of Parauta in the distance (MAP 7). The sheep have made a well-worn path down this grassy/stony slope towards a good-looking path running at right angles at the bottom and a quarry slightly to the left. From the top your direction is initially east, then south past a solitary rock (MAP 8), then south east down a ridge and then left to reach the rough path/track (MAP 9). Turn left and follow the track as it meanders up, down, left and right alongside the working quarry. It then drops down into a valley leaving the quarry behind and you rejoin the path you came up on at MAP 3. Pass through the gate ahead and to your right and retrace your steps back to the starting point.

WALK 106 - BENAOJAN TO RONDA FROM THE CUEVA DEL GATO

Time: 6 hours 20 Kilometres

Difficulty: moderate

Terrain: tracks and paths

BRIEF DESCRIPTION: a fairly gentle walk from the Cueva del Gato, initially along the Guadiaro valley towards Estacion de Benaojan then up and over rolling hills. You pass by the Ermita Virgen de la Cabeza before dropping down to the Guadalevin to return via the GR141/249 along the Guadiaro river. You can start this walk from Ronda - see later in text.

NOTE: in 2018 there was severe flooding in this valley and the bridge accessing the Cueva del Gato was washed away. Before starting the walk check the state of the bridge and the height of the river. If you are not happy about fording the river then it is easy to walk the last section along the road.

HOW TO GET THERE: take the Ronda to Benaojan road and before you reach Estacion de Benaojan, look out for a sign on the right for the Cueva del Gato. Turn down here and park at the bottom in the car park just beyond the ticket office. If you are starting from Ronda. Head out from Barrio San Francisco to the south of the old town on the road to Algeciras. After 1 kilometre on this road, turn right to follow the signs to the Ermita Virgen de la Cabeza and pick the directions at *** in the text

https://es.wikiloc.com/rutas-senderismo/walk-106-from-book-special-walks-in-southern-andalucia-benaojan-to-ronda-from-the-cueva-del-gato-th-33811233

THE WALK: From the car park, follow the river bank downstream for 1400 metres where you pass under a road bridge. Go 150 metres further and turn left up a rough path leading steeply into trees. (MAP 1)

The path doubles back to head north east. It leaves the trees, passing through 2 gates, crosses a stream bed, and then veers right to become a rough track, climbing the open hillside. (MAP 2) After a few metres take the rough path to the left by a cairn. (you can also continue up the track as they meet 150 m further up) Pass a ruin on your right having passed through a gate if you took the rough path. The rough track eventually levels out and follows a sort of ridge with Ronda coming into view in the distance.

The route drops into a valley and becomes a very well-made track and after passing a track to the left, continues in the same direction up the other side. At the top ignore a track to the left and drop down into the next valley. The next section is concreted and halfway up the next hill, you arrive at a junction where there is a panel board explaining that you have come along the Colada Camino de Cortes de la Frontera, an ancient drover's path (MAP 3). Turn left to join the GR 141 and continue up the now tarmacked road to reach the main road at the outskirts of Ronda. Just before the main road turn left down a gravel track signposted to the Ermita (chapel) Virgen de la Cabeza. (MAP 4)

(*** JOIN THE WALK HERE FROM RONDA)

Go 2 kilometres down this track which finishes in a car park with the entrance to the rock cut chapel at the far right hand corner (the chapel is open to the public but with erratic opening hours – the last two occasions the author

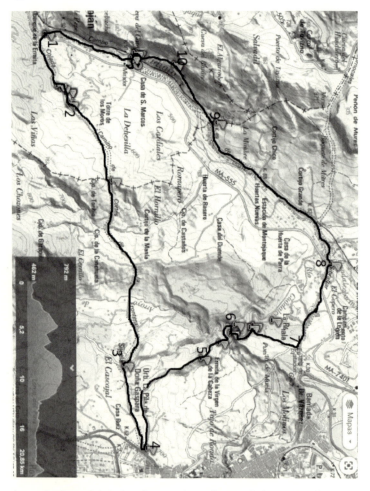

has tried to visit it has been closed). Look for a small metal gate in the left corner (MAP 5). It is easy to climb if padlocked, then follow a rough path alongside the fence on your right which leads you down the ridge to a stream at the bottom.

Cross over and follow an obvious path going diagonally to the right which climbs the steep bank to join a wide track with a splendid farm opposite (MAP 6). Turn right and drop down to cross the river Guadalevin on an ancient bridge with fine brickwork. The grounds of the farm estate are on the left with a magnificent neo-classical gazebo in the rockface. Zigzag up the hill (ignore wikiloc track at this point, rejoins before MAP 8) and after passing a couple of tracks to the right arrive at a cross-roads of tracks. (MAP 7) Turn left to join the GR141/249 and GR7 and go down the hill passing by several houses to meet a road (MA 4701). Turn left to follow the road for about 500 metres and then take an asphalt track to the right as the road bends to the left and before it crosses the river (MAP 8). (If you have decided against fording the river by the Cueva del Gato then just follow the road back to the car)

The track follows the river Guadiaro and when it reaches the railway line turn right to cross the line on a level crossing. Then turn immediately left and go along a dirt track alongside the line for 2.5 kilometres, where you meet a track which has just crossed the railway line (MAP 9). Cross over and continue on a path still following the railway then after 400 metres it leaves the railway to climb up the side of the hill. 600 metres further on take a rough path to the left dropping down the slope towards the river and the Cueva (cave) del Gato. (MAP 10) At the time of writing the bridge over the Guadiaro from the cave, has been swept away by floods in 2018 and is awaiting repair. However the river is easy to ford, unless there have been recent heavy rains. On the other side just pass to the right of the gate by the ticket office where there is a gap in the fence to return to your car.

WALK 107 RONDA - FROM PUERTO LAS ENCINAS BORRACHAS TO THE TAJO ABANICO – RETURN VIA PILAR DE CARTAJIMA

Time: 5 hours (18 Km)

Difficulty: moderate

Terrain: mainly tracks, two sections of rough paths, and some tarmac sections

BRIEF DESCRIPTION: this is one of Ronda's best kept secrets. The Tajo Abanico (the gorge of the fan) is close to Ronda and has a spectacular rock formation caused by the erosion of the Sihuela stream. The GR 141 forms part of the route and the return section passes by the Pilar de Cartajima anda virtually unknown Roman aqueduct. At the start of the walk there are warnings that shooting takes place, so to be safe it is best to avoid Thursdays and weekends between September and March.

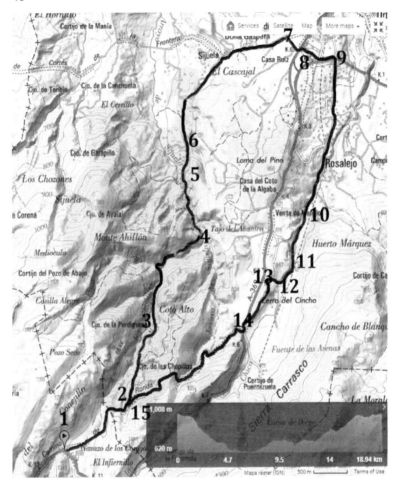

https://www.wikiloc.com/wikiloc/view.do?id=16018232

HOW TO GET THERE: from Ronda take the A369 to Algeciras and 7 kilometres from Ronda at the Puerto de las Encinas Borrachas: park in a layby on the right with a sign for Dolmen de las Encinas Borrachas: from Gaucin drive towards Ronda on the A369 and after passing ALgatocin, Benaladid and Atajate after about 27 kilometres you will arrive at the Puerto de las Encinas Borrachas, the pass of the Drunken Oak trees.

FROM RONDA Follow signs to Algeciras from south of the old town and 150 metres past Bar La Cuadra on the right take a road to the left after the end of the built-up area. Start directions at ***

Just through the gap in the hillside there is a small lay-by on the left where you can park (MAP 1); there is a gate in the fence at the far end leading into a wide open area flanked by a rocky hillside.

THE WALK: A rough track passes through the middle of this open area; this is the GR 141 heading to Ronda. Follow this track, noticing on the left a rather disappointing dolmen together with a sign, without which you would probably pass by unaware of this monument.

After just over a kilometre take the left fork (MAP 2) and soon approach a set of large metal gates. These are usually padlocked but there is a pedestrian access up to the right. Rejoin the track and continue down the hill passing an artificial lake on your left.

 Shortly after you will pass between some farm buildings,

ignoring a track off to the left just before the buildings (MAP 3). Continue down the valley with a stream bed on your left: this becomes the Arroyo Sihuela in due course. The track crosses over the streambed climbing slightly before settling down to follow the left side of the valley. A kilometre after crossing the streambed the track veers off to the right, while you continue straight on down a path (MAP 4).

After about 300 metres you pass through a double gate and the path becomes somewhat rougher as you enter the Tajo de Abanico. (MAP 5)

Take time to enjoy the spectacular rock formations both on the left and right. The path emerges at the far end, climbing up via a metal gate onto a small rocky plateau; 200 metres later it emerges on to a track via another metal gate (MAP 6).

Follow the track for 800 m (10 minutes) and take a right fork uphill at a Y junction. After a further 800 metres (10 minutes) take another right fork at a Y junction and continue for 1 K or about 15 minutes. Look for a rough track going off at right angles on the right side between olive groves (MAP 7). Take this and go 200 metres until the track turns right. Go straight on to follow the side of the field in front of you to reach a road about 50 metres away. Turn left onto the road and go a few metres to turn right down a side road (MAP 8)(*** start point from Ronda). Follow this road for 500 metres until you reach a junction. (MAP 9) Turn right and after crossing over the Ronda by pass continue along this narrow tarmac road past numerous entrances to villas and fincas, ignoring any turn offs for about 20 minutes until you reach the Pilar de Cartajima, a spring and a water trough on the left (MAP 10). The track continues for 400 metres before reaching an entrance to a private house; your route passes to the left along a path (MAP 11). This runs near a stream for 200 metres. At this point look up to your right to try and spot a roman aqueduct, another well-kept secret only recently discovered by the author. (It is not easy to see.) Then the path leaves the stream and gently climbs before arriving at a track and crossing between two wire fences to the other side of the track and then continuing parallel to the track heading south. After 300 metres the path emerges onto a track which is on a hairpin bend (MAP 12). Turn right uphill for 100 metres bearing right on two parallel tracks; take the left-hand of the two tracks and bear left. You will see a pylon ahead just where the track turns sharp right to join the main road.

Take the small path going straight by the pylon; (MAP 13) it soon bears left up the small hill in front of you. Walk along the path which runs parallel to the road for 600 metres before joining a track which leads you to the road. Turn left and go 100 metres before turning right up a rough track heading up the slope (MAP 14). It keeps climbing for 1.5 Kilometres before meeting a Y junction. Take the right fork and continue for a further kilometre where you join the track on which you started the walk. (MAP 15) Turn left and it is 1300 metres back to the road.

WALK 108 - RONDA – SIERRA DE LAS NIEVES – ALCAJONA

Time: 6.5 hours (15 kilometres) (shorter version 13 K and 6 hours)
Difficulty: hard
Terrain: mainly rough paths, mountain side, some track

BRIEF DESCRIPTION: a spectacular walk in the natural park of the Sierra de las Nieves, which takes in two 1500 metre peaks and ridges with great views in all directions.

HOW TO GET THERE: take the A376 Ronda to San Pedro road and turn left into the Parque Natural Sierra de las Nieves between K 137 and 136. Go just over 2 kilometres towards the Area Recreativa Las Quejigales and take the right fork just where the track crosses a stream, signposted to Fuenfria. Drive for just under 4 kilometres and with a farm on your left, park at an area with picnic tables.

THE WALK: at the picnic area where the track splits take the left option and climb up this track for just over 2 kilometres until it meets a ridge coming down from your left. Just before the track starts to descend in zigzags, turn left up a rough path, which immediately edges to the right off the ridge and roughly follows the contour line heading generally north. (MAP 1) After crossing one ridge and then

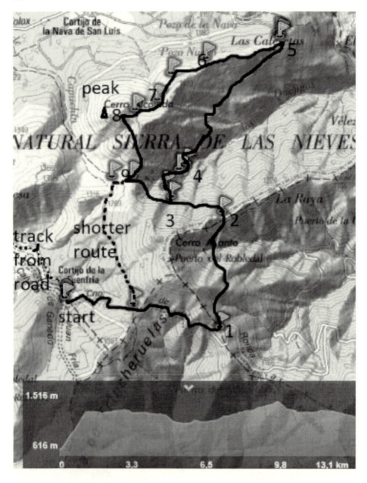

https://es.wikiloc.com/rutas-senderismo/alcojona-sierra-de-las-nieves-34390658

traversing a wide gully, you reach another ridge with a fence running at right angles to your direction. The path splits here. Go straight on through a wire and post gate and turn right to start to lose height. (MAP 2) You are heading along the side of a valley towards a shoulder between 2 peaks. Your heading is more westerly. Just after you traverse a scree covered gully and about 400 metres before the shoulder ahead, locate and turn on to a small path leading down to your right towards the streambed below. (MAP 3)

The path is not easy to follow but bear in mind you will cross the valley below so keep going down the ridge through bushes on the left-hand side of a gully to your right.   I have placed a few cairns which may help. As you approach the stream, take the left fork where the path splits, (MAP 4) cross the stream and then follow the side of the mountain now heading north east and climbing gently. Some 2 kilometres from the streambed you reach a mirador with spectacular views over the valley below and towards the mass of the Torrecilla mountain.

Just left and up from the mirador, turn left at a junction of paths (MAP 5). Just a few metres further on, a cairn marks a small path to the right leading to a massive pinsapo tree known as the Punto de la Mesa. You can pass to the left of the tree to pick up cairns marking the rocky route along the ridge, or return to the main path to continue round the corner and up through rocks to the same spot where cairns mark the route.

Follow along the ridge with the best path just to the left, with cairns at intervals to guide you. Cross over to the right-hand side when the grassy ledges to the left peter out (MAP 6) and then start climbing the mountain ahead keeping on the right-hand side of the ridge, using goat paths as they appear.

Pass through a small coppice of pines (MAP 7) and then approach a gully separating the peak of Alcajona to your right from the main ridge to your left. When you reach the gully cross over and climb the rough ground to reach the summit marked by a large cairn, from which you get great views of Ronda and the Grazalema mountains beyond (MAP 8) (The wikiloc track runs straight up the gully and misses out the peak).

Return to the main ridge and continue in the same direction (due south) to descend the ridge to a shoulder below, where there are pine trees. When you reach the flatter shoulder (MAP 9), there is a path off to the left down the steep slope and will lead you some 400 metres to the junction of paths at MAP3 where you came in the opposite direction earlier in the walk. You will temporarily leave the wikiloc track until you reach MAP 3. The wikiloc follows the shorter route. – see below **.

Now it is a matter of retracing your steps to the wire and post gate, crossing over the ridge and following the path back to the track and turning right to rejoin your car.

** (If you wish to shorten the walk then at the shoulder, you can climb the rather high fence where it is fastened to a pine tree and head west down the slope for 200 metres, turn left onto a track and follow it back to the main track to turn right to rejoin your car. This is private land but you are most unlikely to meet anyone. The wikiloc track goes this way.

WALK 109 – CARTAJIMA TO PUJERRA- RETURN VIA JUZCAR

Time: 5 hours (15 kilometres)
Difficulty: hard due to height gain
Terrain: track then path up to Pujerra, track then paths to Juzcar, and a path/track back to Cartajima

BRIEF DESCRIPTION: A fabulous walk involving a descent and ascent on two occasions into the valley of the Genal and a visit to three villages of the Alto Genal. One tricky piece of navigation and a river crossing. The last section is up a beautiful valley on a quiet path recently restored and marked up by the Juzcar Town hall. This walk is one of the best kept secrets of the Serrania de Ronda.

HOW TO GET THERE: from Ronda take the road to San Pedro (A 376) and after 8 kilometres from the new hospital turn right signposted Cartajima and Igualeja. Then turn right again on MA 7306 to Cartajima. When you reach the village park at the entrance which is a road to the left of the MA7306.

PROFILE

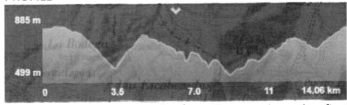

THE WALK: walk towards the village and at the first opportunity turn right to take a concrete road round the side of the village. It drops down to a junction. (the wikilocs track starts here, and you can also leave your car here.) Turn right and follow a track heading along the

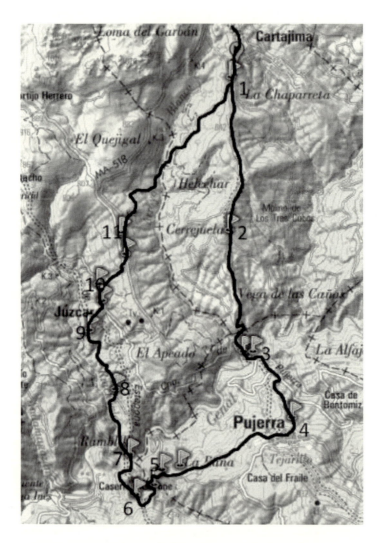

https://www.wikiloc.com/hiking-trails/walk-109-from-book-special-walks-in-southern-andalucia-cartajima-to-pujerra-return-via-juzcar-34908259 ridge heading south on the PR- A – 225 ignoring the track to the right which is the PR -A-224 your return route (MAP 1). This track will take you all the way to Pujerra. The way down the hill to the Genal valley is straightforward, apart being alert to take the middle track where the track splits three ways, 1300 metres from the village (MAP 2). At the bottom you join a road (Juzcar to Pujerra) turning left to cross the Rio Genal.

 A few metres further on (MAP 3), leave the road to take a path to the left marked by yellow and white flashes, which leads steeply uphill into woods. After a few minutes you cross the road to continue up the path until you arrive at the lower end of Pujerra. There is an excellent view-point and a bench to recover from the climb (MAP 4) (Mirador de la Cruz. Continue into the village on the same concrete road leaving the mirador to your right. After you have entered the village, take the second street on the right (Calle Esperon) and your heading is now due west on a concrete track which leaves the village on the level to begin with and then gently descends into chestnut woods. Pass through metal gates and after 25 minutes or so (just under 2 kilometres) as the track does a right hand turn look for a rough track to the left leading down to a small concrete water reservoir (MAP 5). Pass to the left and then turn immediately right to walk along the wall of the reservoir. (If you are following the wikiloc track ignore the track to the left where the author went wrong!) The path now enters trees and descends a ridge, zig-zagging down into the steep gorge below. Careful navigation is needed as the bushes have grown over in places to make the path difficult to locate. NB after 150 metres make sure you keep right where there is a choice of paths. Near the bottom pass through a wire and post gate, then cross the stream and keep left at a grassy area. Head upstream for a few metres, then turn sharp right up the hill to reach a gate 200 metres later which leads to a footpath coming down the hill (MAP 6). Turn right, down the ridge to follow the blue arrowed path to meet a track at the bottom which leads to a finca to the left. (the substantial building below on your left is a former tin factory, now a winery)

Cross over the track and follow a rough path along the bank of the stream which leads to the banks of the river Genal. Manoeuvre through the bushes to get to the river. (MAP 7) Edge left a few metres, cross over and the path is opposite. (the bridge was washed away in the 2018 floods) Follow the path as it rises up the hill. You are still on the blue marked path which will take you up to Juzcar. Ignore one track to the left as you cross a gully and keep on the path which goes straight up the other side through a broken-down gate (MAP 8). When you reach a fork keep right (MAP 9) and head up a steep concrete track which soon comes to the outskirts of the village of Juzcar. Take the first street to the left (Calle Fuente Carailla) and keep right at the next fork to reach the main road running through the village. Turn left and pass by a couple of bars and then at the next corner turn right up a steep concrete track to pass houses (MAP 10) and then leave the village. After 10 minutes emerge on the main road. Turn left and go 200 metres up the road and take the first path down to the right – the PR – A – 224 to Cartajima (MAP 11). This is a straightforward section where you first drop down to the valley then rise up the other side through chestnut groves to reach the bottom end of the village, where you began the walk.

WALK 110 - MONTEJAQUE/BENAOCAZ VENTANA MOUNTAIN CIRCUIT

Time: 6 hours (14 Kilometres)
Difficulty: Hard, due to rough going and climbing
Terrain: road, track and path, with a large part over open country

BRIEF DESCRIPTION: a spectacular walk up the 1300 metre peak of La Ventana. There is a lot of open rocky country side with a lack of paths and is best done with the help of the wikiloc track. An anti-clockwise circular walk via the villages of Montejaque and Benaojan.

HOW TO GET THERE: from Benoajan/Montejaque take the road to Cortes (MA 8401) and 1.5 kilometres from the junction park in the small car park on the left overlooking Benaojan. 30 metres downhill on the left is the start of the walk.

PROFILE

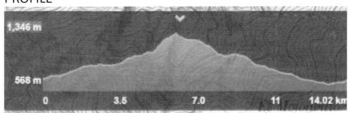

THE WALK: start the walk at the panelboard indicating the path to the Llano de Libar which you will initially follow. Head between buildings uphill on a track zigzagging after 50 metres, then take the left hand option heading south to soon pass farm buildings to join a better track. Then pass through or to the left of a metal gate and as the track turns sharp left to drop down to the road, go straight on through a metal gate ahead and on to a path climbing the

FIRST PART OF WALK

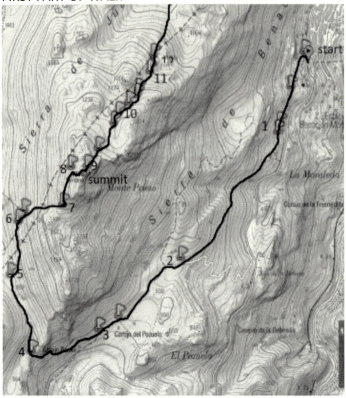

https://www.wikiloc.com/hiking-trails/walk-110-from-book-special-walks-in-andalucia-ventana-circuit-from-benaojan-to-montejaque-circuit-34059792

hill parallel to the road (MAP 1). 1300 metres later you join a track where you turn right (MAP 2). The track enters a plain and you pass close by a watering hole on your right to pass through a metal gate. 100 metres later you leave the track veering right onto a rough path heading diagonally up the side of the mountain (MAP 3).

There is a rickety wooden sign indicating Llano de Libar. The surface becomes paved with stones further up.

You will reach a kind of ledge where the path changes direction to north and climbs a gully. (MAP 4) Ignore any paths to the left, and head to the top of the gully. This is the Puerto Pozuelo. Just past a flat grassy area and as you enter another grassy area, locate a metal-rodded gate in the fence to the right. (MAP 5) Go through and then follow cairns diagonally to the left on the side of the mountain, keeping the fence to your left but in sight. You will rejoin it at one point if you are following the wikiloc track. (the cairns are helpful here as there are a mass of ill-defined goat paths for the next 500 metres) At a point where the fence is broken down and then turns left and loses height, (MAP 6) leave the fence and head straight uphill eastwards for 500 metres on a goat path up a grassy gully marked with an occasional cairn to continue your ascent of the Ventana in an easterly direction.

When you reach a shoulder, (MAP 7) veer left, marked by several cairns and head due north keeping to the left side of the peak following a grassy ledge. and after about 300 metres you can turn right (MAP 8) heading east and aim up to the trig point marking the summit which you will see a few metres further up. The directions from here like many peaks are not an exact science: common sense and a sense of direction is all that is needed. You will have to scramble up the rocks. Enjoy the views at the top (MAP 9). You will see Ronda, the peaks of Torrecilla to the east and Reloj and Simancon to the west as well as down the Llano de Libar.

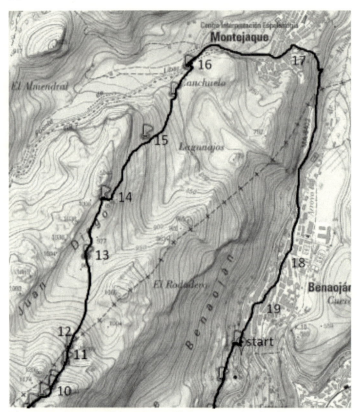

The way down will be generally in a northerly direction, but initially head down the rocks to the east and where there is a flattish area. Use the grassy ledges and gullies to aid your descent. (there are cairns here) Once off the rocky slabs you enter a flatter area, less rocky and with sparse vegetation. Your aim is to head due north between two parallel ridges. Pass along a shallow gully, then as you reach a small grassy hollow veer right (if using wikilocs ignore a brief diversion to your left) and briefly climb up between a gap in the rocks (cairn here) and pass down this gully to a fence (MAP 10).

Cross over or under in a suitable place, (there are places where gaps have been made or you can lift the barbed wire to make a space) then continue north down a gully on the roughest of goat paths marked by the occasional cairn. 200 metres from the fence your way is apparently blocked by a low rock face in front of you (MAP 11). Here you turn left and follow a rough path along the left side of the gully towards a gap in the mountainside ahead and below. There is a rock with a prominent cairn in the gap (MAP 12). Pass through and continue your descent leaving a prominent circular threshing floor to your right.

You now reach the lower end of a long glacial type valley running south west - north east with peaks and ridges on either side. (MAP 13) Cross over the grassy bottom heading north and through a gap in the ridge to your right. A valley opens out in front of you and you will see Montejaque below to the north east (MAP 14).

There is a path of sorts on the west side of the valley stained brown from constant use by sheep and goats so it should be easy to follow as it also uses the natural rock structures running down the left hand side of the valley heading north-east. From the top of the valley until you leave via a low gap to your left, it is just under 2 kilometres. At one point (MAP 15) you veer right briefly before resuming your general northerly direction. As you approach a ridge ahead of you, start to veer left towards this gap, (you join various goat paths coming from your right and a path will lead you down through the rocks via a gate to a track below (MAP 16).

Turn right and at the next junction take the right-hand track heading down the hill into Montejaque which becomes the Calle Dr Vasquez y Gutierrez. Go into the main square (Plaza de la Constitucion) then leave the hotel to your right along the Calle Nueva, and take the first street to the right, then left down Calle Manuel Ortega. After 50 metres turn right down a narrow street (MAP 17) which drops down the hill and leaves the village with a rocky hillside to the right and above. After a few zigzags it reaches the road below. Turn right and follow the road into Benaojan ignoring the road to Cortes on your right up which your car is parked.

Just past a supermarket there is a Y junction with a mini roundabout (MAP 18). Fork right along Calle Presbitero Jose Moreno and continue along this street until you reach the rather ugly modern town hall on your left (MAP 19). Leave the square at the top left corner along Calle Fuente heading south. Beyond the church, turn right uphill then left to join Calle La Linea and after about 300 metres you will reach a road. Turn left to rejoin your car.

WALK 111 MONTEJAQUE - SIERRA DE MONTALITE

Time: 5 hours 18 kilometres
Difficulty: medium
Terrain: paths and tracks, some cross-country work

BRIEF DESCRIPTION: a very pleasant walk in wild unspoilt countryside passing only one or two isolated farms in the Parque Natural De Grazalema.

HOW TO GET THERE: Montejaque can be approached from Benaojan or from the Ronda Sevilla road A 376. At the junction of the two roads into Montajaque, head out north on the MA 8403 for 300 metres then park at the start of a wide track to the left where there are a couple of panel boards.

THE WALK: continue up the track climbing a little for 5 minutes then veer west to enter the attractive valley of the Guadares stream. Frequent panel boards give information about the area as this part is a popular local walk. After 30 minutes as you pass a track leading down to the right take a rough track to the left a few metres further on (MAP 1).

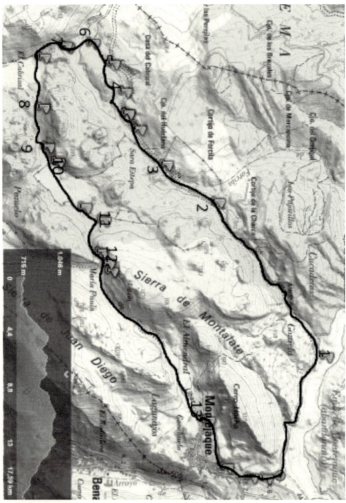
Wikiloc track

https://es.wikiloc.com/rutas-senderismo/book-5-walk-111-montejaque-sierra-montalite-32327076

You now start to climb through olive groves then into wilder scenery through a gate and 1500 metres after the gate, reach a pass with a cattle grid (MAP 2). Now descend into the next valley keeping on the main track and then climb again passing one turn to Cortijo Huerfano. You now approach two gates (MAP 3). Take the left-hand gate and on the other side follow a long wall on your left on a grassy track. After 700 metres from the previous gate pass through a metal gate and continue along the grassy track to the next gate 600 metres further on. (MAP 4) (the wikilocs track leaves the track heading left but rejoins at the gate) If the gate is padlocked then it is easy to climb over to the side.

Continue on the track the other side, passing an attractive stone cottage with a stone table and chairs on the grass outside, and after 500 metres, just as you cross a streambed, go left off the track and scramble under the fence where it crosses over the streambed (MAP 5). Follow the streambed on either side and you will reach a faint grassy track crossing in front of you as you approach the mountain side ahead (MAP 6). Turn left and follow it as it heads up the grassy slope towards the cliffs now heading east. It reduces to a path, enters woods and arrives at a fence where there is a ladder stile which you use to climb over the fence. (MAP 7) Now climb steeply, veering left to pass through a wire and post gate and then pass along the side of a grassy hollow to your left.

The path now enters a large grassy plain (Llano de Zurraque). Once in the plain head south east to a tree studded rocky outcrop jutting out into the plain, keep it to your left and head northeast to locate a path marked by cairns (MAP 8) which will lead you eastwards for about 1 kilometre, through trees, bushes and rocks to a pass between the surrounding outcrops. The path inevitably meanders as there are many obstacles. (The wikiloc track goes about 50 metres further to your left also following cairns but not on such a clear path)

When you arrive at the pass there is a wall in front of you and another plain ahead and below. (MAP 9) Bear left and the path follows the wall on your right. At the end of the wall, pass through a metal gate (MAP 10) and head into the plain leaving a watering hole to your right and follow a grassy track heading north east. The track enters woods and a few minutes later reaches a junction with a small fenced hollow on your right (MAP 11). Turn right up a good track and as the track flattens out after a gentle climb, take a rough path down to the left marked by a cairn, (MAP 12) past some feeding troughs towards a gully. Aim for the fence to your right and 100 metres down there is a gate leading on to a good track.

Turn left onto the track and follow it down a majestic valley for 2 kilometres to the outskirts of Montejaque, below and to your right. When you reach a fork, (MAP 13) keep left on a concrete road which after rising briefly, drops steeply down into the village. Turn left at the bottom and go 300 metres down a street until you reach a road. Turn left and 200 metres later you will rejoin your car.

WALK 112 - MONTEJAQUE LLANO DE LIBAR AND LLANO DE REPUBLICANO

Time: 5.5 hours 18.5 kilometres
Difficulty: moderate
Terrain: tracks, rocky paths, open country

BRIEF DESCRIPTION: a fine walk with rewarding views over the Sierra de Grazalema and the Sierra de Libar. There is relatively little height gain and a reasonable amount of flat track. You can start from Montejaque, Villaluenga (an extra 6 Kilometres) or Grazalema.

HOW TO GET THERE: Montejaque can be approached from Benaojan or from the Ronda Sevilla road A 376. At the junction of the two roads into Montajaque, head out north on the MA 8403 for 100 metres then turn sharp left up a side street (Av Europa) and after 300 metres turn right up a steep concrete road (Calle Libar) which leads out into the countryside. After 1 kilometre as the road drops downhill and meets a track coming up from the left from the village, go straight on up the valley on a very rough track for just under 6 kilometres, passing a farm on your right, then go through a gate and just after you enter woods and the track starts to rise find a place to park near a wide path and a metal gate on the right as the track bends to the left.

STARTING FROM VILLALUENGA: from Villaluenga take a concrete road from the north end of the village signposted as the GR 7 to Montejaque. Park at the top of the hill and continue on the GR 7 which now drops down the hill the other side for 1700 metres where it passes through a gate and then turns left off the track after 300 metres to cross open land towards a steep rocky cliff face.

When you reach the start of the cliffs join the walk instructions at ** where you turn left.

FROM GRAZALEMA: on the Grazalema – Ronda road A372, just past the turn off A374 to Villaluenga, take the first track to the right by a venta (Meson Los Alamos) then after 50 metres take the left fork. 1200 metres from the road fork right and 4 kilometres from the road park your car at a junction where a rough track leaves to the left, just before a rocky outcrop. This start point is recommended if you are worried about your car on the rough track from Montejaque.
Join the walk directions at ***

THE WALK: (starting from Montejaque) continue along the track you have just driven in on; (this is the GR7 long distance foot path) it climbs a little more, then settles to run along a valley with steep slopes either side. 2.5 kilometres from the start, take the right fork when the track splits and the bear left 200 metres later, where a track to the right leads to a building which is a refuge for overnight stops. (MAP 1)

The track continues along the Llano (plain) de Libar and 700 metres later, keep straight on along a grassy track. After a further kilometre pass through a gate and then approach a wall belonging to a farmstead ahead and to the left. (MAP 2) You edge right on a path keeping the wall to your left which heads towards a gap in the mountainside (The Puerto de los Correos); you are still on the GR7 and signs will assist. Head up to the pass and after passing through a gate you will reach a panel board relating to the GR7. (MAP 3)

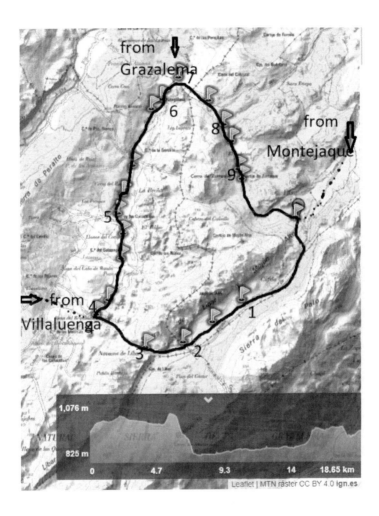

https://www.wikiloc.com/hiking-trails/walk-book-5-walk-112-llano-de-libar-puerto-de-correo-llano-de-republicano-zurraque-46111509

Pass by and the rocky path crosses over the pass and drops down the other side. At a flatter section you pass a finger post and a path leading to a ruin on your left before the GR7 drops steeply down again to the bottom of the steep mountainside and a large flat grassy plain.

Pass through a gate in a wall (MAP 4) and turn immediately right (** Join the walk coming from Villaluenga here) and then follow the wall with a streambed on your left until you reach the impressive Sima del Republicano 500 metres further on, which is where the stream goes into an underground system via a cave and pothole.

Then, still heading north, cross another streambed and follow this stream with the wall still on your right. A kilometre from the Sima cross another streambed and then pass through a gate. After a further 500 metres pass through another gate and keep heading north on a faint grassy track. The track passes to the left of a farm building and reaches a junction (MAP 5). Turn right and continue until you reach a padlocked gate across the track. Turn right down the fence and 50 metres later turn left through a gate, then go 2 kilometres along a grassy track passing through 2 more gates along the way. 300 metres after the second gate cross over a stream via a bridge (MAP 6) and go immediately left and then up a bank to turn left on to a gravel track as it heads north to the left of a rocky outcrop for 600 metres. At this point the track continues north while you turn right (MAP 7) onto a rougher track which

(*** join the walk from Grazalema at this point turning left up the track.)

heads east keeping the rocky ridge parallel on your right. You also follow a stream on your right, the arroyo de los Alamos. After passing through 2 gates, a kilometre from the last turn off and 100 metres on from the second gate leave the track to your left (MAP 8) and cross open ground after fording the stream and head for the corner of the two rocky ridges which converge ahead of you.

Look for a ladder stile in a fence to your right, climb it and start climbing the side of the slope and immediately passing through a wire and post gate towards the low part of the range. A rough path will lead you by a sunken area to your left and then you will see a flat grassy area with scattered trees ahead. Enter this plain and keep to the right-hand edge towards a white building in the distance. and head south for about 600 metres when you will pass by a large well and some abandoned farm buildings to your left.

Go just 50 metres beyond the well into the trees slightly to the right and at the start of a slope to locate a metal gate, (MAP 9) pass through and follow the path the other side. After about 200 metres veer right onto an earthy track and passes through woods along the valley floor at one point veering left to the north and then east to reach the track through a metal gate where your car is parked .

WALK 113   CORTES – THE SCULPTURES WALK

Time: 6.5 hours   (16.5 Kilometres)
Difficulty: hard due to scramble and rough paths.
Terrain: Mainly rough paths, one section of rocky scrambling, a short section of good track at the start and finish of the walk

BRIEF DESCRIPTION: a spectacular walk in the Sierra de Libar above Cortes using a little-known path along the top of the Sierra de Libar with great views down both the Llano de Libar and the Llano del Republicano.

HOW TO GET THERE: Drive to Cortes de la Frontera and from the bullring follow the directions north to the MA549 towards Jimera de Libar and Ronda. At a small roundabout just outside the town turn left up to the instituto (secondary school), there is a Parque Natural sign to 'Los Llanos. Leave the instituto to your left; the track becomes gravelled and park on the wider part of the track by a small paddock and barn.
 THE WALK: walk up the track a short way, it is concreted to begin with. Just before a red metal gate turn off right onto a stony path which is marked by a waymark post with faded yellow and white bands and follow uphill until it meets the track again. Turn right onto the track and follow it uphill. As it turns to concrete and bends sharp right bear left up a rough path which comes back to the track opposite an old finca and a spring (fuente) with a drinking water trough. 30 metres further on, when the track turns right take a path on the left marked with green blobs of paint. (MAP 1) Follow this path uphill until you meet the track again, (this cuts off another loop of the driveable

MAP 1 FIRST AND LAST PART OF WALK 113

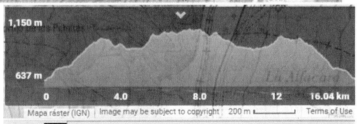

track although in fact this loop is not much longer and it is an easier walk either uphill or downhill).

You arrive once more at the track, turn left onto this track, (the junction is marked with a yellow/white marker) and soon you arrive at a small col with a choice of tracks. (MAP 2)

The main left-hand track, which winds uphill, is signposted "Los Pinos" on a stone; turn right here between a large cairn on your left and a pile of white gravel on your right, then immediately take the left fork which is a rough path. After 3 minutes you reach a wire and post gate. Pass through the gate and follow the stony path for 10 minutes or so. There is a large circular 'llano' below on the left.

The stony path, marked from time to time with green blobs of paint passes over a ridge and heads to a grassy track ahead. Turn left and follow slightly downhill to start with then after 200 metres, turn sharp left to drop into a grassy hollow (MAP 3). You are heading towards a small finca you can see ahead on the far side. Cross the circular grassy area to the abandoned finca called Cortijo de Edmundo (MAP 4).

https://www.wikiloc.com/hiking-trails/walk-112-from-walk-book-40-special-walks-in-southern-andalucia-cortes-de-la-frontera-sculptures-23793126

MAP 2 WALK 113

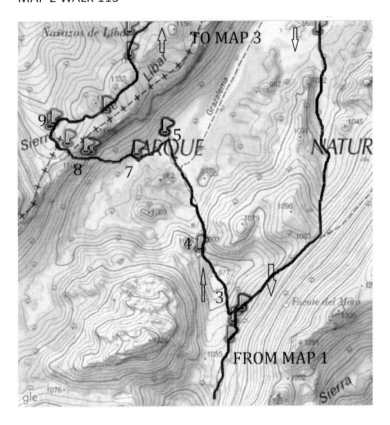

Beyond the finca, go through a "pass" in the rocks and follow the stony path around a huge boulder. The stony path comes out at the bottom, then passes between a few rocks and trees and to the left hidden in the trees a 'sima' – a scary and vast deep fissure in the ground – take care!!

Head across the flat ground towards an animal enclosure; Go through the metal panelled gate, head to the end of the large corral and on the right there is a pallet you can use as a stile to climb the wall. (MAP 5) Follow the wall round to the left and join a grassy track (there is a spring and water trough to the right), which passes through a wire and post gate in the fence ahead. At this point you are heading south with massive cliffs on your right. Your next stage is to climb these cliffs but up a less steep looking section and 30 degrees to your right.

Walk a short way past some large piles of stones, look up to the right to see a large boulder on the top of the cliff face, which looks like an oddly shaped 'football'. Just after here you come to some large rocks; here head up right and diagonally to the corner, there is no path apart from animal tracks (MAP 7).

Head for the corner at 45 degrees from the track you have left; ahead there is a fence and your aim is to get into a gully just below the steep part of the rock face where there is a fallen branch over the gully making an arch. (the wikiloc track gets to the fence a little low so it is better to keep to the right of the wikiloc track until you reach the gully) At the top of the gully there is the fence, (MAP 8) pass through where it has been cut by hunters, then climb up the rocks, steeply uphill with some clambering required – you are trying to follow an animal route (the stones/rocks are discoloured with brown) up to the col where you can pass through a small gap to then drop down the other side towards a flat area. Now follow a vague path downhill, keeping in a fairly straight direction past a couple of cairns and an upright 'sculpture' to a 'T junction' by a large white rock and a cairn.

Turn right by this cairn, just go a few metres and turn right by large single "sculpted "rock (MAP 9). This is where the sculptures path begins, named because some individual has taken considerable trouble to mark the path with unusually shaped rocks. During the next hour along the undulating heights of the Sierra de Libar, the path is reasonably well-marked by a brown discolouration on the rocks, and a number of limestone 'sculptures' and cairns. It just needs a certain amount of concentration to ensure you remain on the right path.

Look out for the following landmarks: (wikilocs will greatly help on this section as there are frequent waymark photos)

- Almost immediately there is a grassy area where the path is a little unclear - bear left and then almost immediately climb up the bank on your right to pick up the path again. (Cairns will help)

- After an area with large rocks where you go up over a 'pass' and then down the other side, you come to a 'T' junction. Here turn left (if you go right it goes to a viewing spot over the llano).

- At a more open area where the path is again a little indistinct, go up and right.

- Over a rocky scree, then down through the woods.

- You get to a rocky 'top' then go through woods again.

- ☐ A flatter grassy area, go straight on the good path (a view to the left).

- ☐ When you meet a stone wall ahead with a cairn, turn right. There are larger rocks on your right.

- ☐ A more open area with cut-out rock pools on the right and a large cairn. Here go uphill (keeping the pools behind you and to the right).

- ☐ Up right between rocks, sculpture on the left. A good path.

- ☐ An animal head! and a few metres later you'll see a pelvis on a tree!

- ☐ More sculptures.

- ☐ Down to a flat grassy area which can be a little wet by the valley floor where the path becomes less marked; at the end of this valley section, the path goes uphill to the left (look for a cairn which marks the path winding uphill between rocks on both sides).

At the top of this section, leave the main route and bear right to a good lunch spot (views over the llano). **3¼ hours to here.** (MAP 10)

After the lunch spot, return to the main route where you head for a tall thin upright rock ahead. After this thin

MAP 3 WALK 113

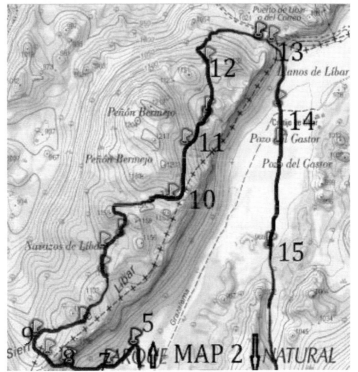

upright rock, follow a zig-zag path, which goes downhill to follow the side of the mountain with views over the Llano to the right and then flattens out a bit and follows the contours.

Start looking for the horse sculpture. (photo in wikilocs) When you get to a small fork by the horse sculpture cairn on your left *(see photograph)* take the right fork, which goes slightly downhill (MAP 11). The llano is on your right. Zig-zag down again to a T-junction and a large rock cairn. Turn right towards another cairn and some jagged rocks straight ahead. Take care, the path is a little unclear but go left just before the jagged rocks at the back of a grassy area to pick up the good path again. You are now climbing steadily, and now start looking for the wall on the ridge, ahead and above you. When you see the wall close by, go uphill to it and climb over the wall just to the right of a bit of wire fencing (MAP 12).

From the wall pick up a good path which zig-zags down the hill. There are a couple of tricky bits where the way is not so clear, but don't stray too far - keep looking out for the good zig-zag path (muddy stones) marked by the occasional cairn. I.e. you need to zig and zag if the path becomes unclear. You are basically constantly heading downhill edging right to enter the lower area, which is the Puerto del Correo through which passes the GR7.

At one point there are three tall sculptures in a row, and then near the bottom the path turns right (no other option) and a little further on you pass a very large rock/cairn. Just after this large rock/cairn bear slightly left downhill and you come out at the bottom on the GR7, by a cairn and four trees close together. Turn right onto the GR7 (a well-used and marked path) and follow it across the grassy plateau until you reach a junction with a large signboard and a signpost saying 'Villalengua 1 hr 45 mins). *4½ hours to the signboard.*
From the signboard pass through the gate beyond and follow a rocky path for a short while (this is the GR7). After only 5 minutes or so leave the GR7 (which goes to Montejaque) and pass through another gate on the right (MAP 13).
 From the gate go immediately left and downhill leaving the drystone wall on your left, to the flat llano below, bearing diagonally right as you descend.

You are now at the bottom of the llano; there are farm buildings opposite – the Cortijo de Libar (2 or 3 white buildings with terracotta roofs). Turn right along a wide track, which goes along the right side of the plain (MAP 14). When these buildings are to your left and at right angles, head diagonally left across the plain to the far LH corner. Cross a small stream, head for a lone tree, and then to a large triangle shaped rock on the right which will start to become more pronounced as you approach it. Go towards a drystone wall you can see ahead and pass through a wire and post gate in the wall (MAP 16). Immediately after the gate, go across a small grassy area then keep to the far left and go uphill, passing between rocks on either side. There are no markings at first, but soon the stony path becomes easier to follow – there are discoloured rocks, and occasional cairns and blobs of green paint. You are climbing steadily but also pass through some flatter, grassy areas, occasionally marked with cairns.

Then the rocky path begins to climb more steeply – you are climbing up the V of a valley, up to the 'col' or saddle you can see uphill and ahead. Once up and over the pass, keep following the stony path around to the right, then slightly down to skirt the side of the hill. From the rocky pass, it then flattens out and passes above the grassy hollow and the finca you passed earlier in the walk (MAP 3).
You meet the original grassy track which you follow making sure you turn right off it after 200 metres and join the rocky path back down the hillside, retracing your route downhill back to the car.

WALK 114 CORTES – GARGANTA DE LAS PULGAS

Time: 4 hours (11 kilometres)
Difficulty: easy
Terrain: tracks and paths, some indistinct

BRIEF DESCRIPTION: an attractive walk in the Alcornocales Natural Park mainly through woodland, not too strenuous. You are recommended to use the wikiloc track which has useful waymarks at key points.

HOW TO GET THERE: from Cortes de la Frontera take the Ubrique road A373 and after 4.5 kilometres (after K 51) take a track to the left and park here.

THE WALK: continue along the forestry track by the display panel for about 600 metres where you turn right (MAP 1) off the track heading for a small farm called Casa del Santo. 400 metres down the track just before you reach the farm, turn left by the boundary wall and where there is a padlocked metal gate (MAP 2). You descend through woods on an ill-defined path keeping the wall/fence on your right, then through an open area then through more woods heading west. The path is not always clear. Keep on through the woods until you reach a fence beyond which is the stream La Pulga in the walk title (MAP 3).
Veer left and follow the fence downstream for just under one kilometre keeping it to your right and at (MAP 4) turn to the left up the slope on a path heading east. Go 200 metres and as you approach a fence with open ground beyond, turn right on to a rough track now heading south (MAP 5).

500 metres later, as the track bends to the left, continue straight on along a less used track (MAP 6) for 400 metres where you join a better track heading south for just 100 metres and as it veers sharply to the left you continue straight on (MAP 7) to follow the white arrows of the official Sendero de la Pulga. The path heads down hill and forks left marked with an arrow (MAP 8) then arrives at a large pond (laguna) (may be dry in the summer months). There is a sign marking the end of the trail.

Continue in the same direction taking the left-hand path a few metres beyond the pond which leads to the road below (MAP 9). Turn right and go 500 metres along the road and take the first track to your left (MAP 10). (The wikilocs track goes left after a few metres through bushes down to the track below, cutting off the corner). You go parallel to the Garganta de la Pulga to your right heading south east for just over a kilometre. The track turns east and after 400 metres keep left where the track forks (MAP 11). Keep going east for another 600 metres passing farm buildings over to the right then fork left uphill heading north, (MAP 12) to join a forestry track just past another farm (MAP 13) still heading north to reach the road after 500 metres (MAP 14).

Turn right, go 200 metres and as the road curves to the right, turn left (MAP 15) up a steep path to head first north west along very indistinct paths along the contour line through scrubby bushes for 150 metres and when you meet a more obvious path running at right angles to your direction turn right to follow it up the slope heading north for about 100 metres making sure you veer left to join a forestry track above you, where you turn right and it is now 700 metres along the track back to your car.

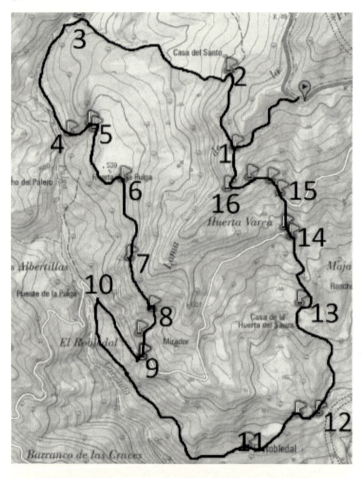

https://www.wikiloc.com/walking-trails/book-5-walk-114-cortes-de-la-frontera-garganta-de-las-pulgas-30766714

WALK 115- ATAJATE TO JIMERA DE LIBAR RETURN VIA LOMO DE LAS MORILLAS

Time: 4.5 hours (10 Kilometres)

Difficulty: hard due to rough terrain

Terrain: paths and tracks, but a long section on very rough sometimes steep, overgrown goat paths

BRIEF DESCRIPTION: A spectacular walk, experience needed as there is much cross country navigation. The first part is straightforward down the very beautiful PR 258 footpath. You pass through the pretty village of Jimera de Libar and return, along a more-or-less extinct unmarked path, hard to follow and traverses a couple of steep sided gorges. The wilderness is hard to beat.

HOW TO GET THERE: just south of Atajate on the A369 Ronda to Gaucin road park opposite the road to Jimera (MA 8307) in the Venta El Paisaje car park. (you may wish to take a drink after the walk)

THE WALK: cross over and go 50 metres down the Jimera road and then leave the road to follow the PR258 and the Ruta Fray Leopoldo. (MAP 1) CARE as you almost immediately fork left down a path off the track leading to a farm. You now follow this path which leads through several bedstead gates and then passes over the ridge and down to a gully to cross a stream bed (MAP 2). On the other side the path climbs and converts to a track which passes through fincas and then drops down to the road. (MAP 3) Turn right and go a few metres and leave the road at the signpost.

Go about 100 metres down this track and then turn left down a path where there is a marker post (MAP 4). Rejoin the road and turn right to enter the village. Just past a water fountain/washhouse, take the first street to the right which leads up to the village square. (MAP 5)

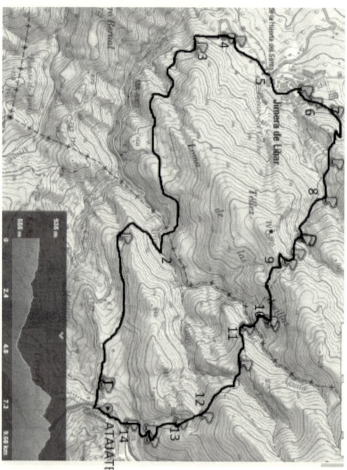

https://www.wikiloc.com/hiking-trails/atajate-jimera-on-pr-258-return-via-morillas-walk-115-from-book-special-walks-in-southern-andalucia-33653374

Go under an archway and turn right up Calle Larga. 200 metres up veer left and then take a steep concrete ramp to the right with a sign to Mirador Las Canchas (MAP 6). This becomes a gravel track and 200 metres later take the right fork uphill (MAP 7). Then keep left now on a paved path. This rounds the hill to the right and flattens out into a wider path. Look ahead and observe a long gully passing up a steep line of cliffs. This is your route for the next 30 minutes or so. The wide path reduces to a narrow path dropping into a gully running at right angles to the one ahead of you. It arrives at a grassy area with a fenced off farm building on your left and peters out. (MAP 8) Go straight on and cross a streambed to enter a long gully. There is the semblance of a path running up near the streambed which also runs up the gully. You now climb following whatever paths you can find. Occasional cairns will provide reassurance. When you reach a rocky outcrop in front of you, it is possible to pass to the left and then veer right again, or you can keep to the right. The gully splits and a separate one goes up to the left. Make sure you keep up the main gully heading roughly east. Then you should edge up on to the ridge and at the top there is a grassy plateau. (MAP 9) Your course is now towards the next gully/gorge in front of you in a south east direction. There is a rough goat path marked with cairns keeping on the right side of a ridge heading down slightly towards a wide ledge. At the top of this ledge head to the right (MAP 10) and follow cairns down the rocky slope to the bottom of the gorge, making sure you note the whereabouts of a steep narrow path climbing up the other side. Take care here as it is steep with loose rocks and stones.

Once across the streambed take the narrow path marked by a cairn and climb out of the gorge heading south up to the ridge. Once on the ridge (MAP 11) turn left to head east along a rough path. Keep to the right of the ridge as you near the top and then you will come to another ridge running at right angles. Ahead of you is another gully and at this point observe a fence and the line of a track 200 metres up the opposite slope. Your aim is to reach this fence. Head down through the bushes (there are one or two rough goat paths to choose from). Cross over at the bottom and go straight up the other side and you will join a well-used goat path heading right and south east.

This leads up to the fence. It now follows the fence until it reaches a shoulder and then turns left through a gap in the rocks and plunges downhill (MAP 12). Follow the path down the gully (rough going in places and ending up in a streambed and through a gate at the bottom by a finca to your right up a track, which you cross over to reach the road via an almond grove (MAP 14). Turn right to rejoin your car at the Venta 200 metres further on.

WALK 116 – BENADALID TO ATAJATE AND RETURN VIA EL SOTILLO

Time: 4.5 hours (15.5 kilometres)
Difficulty: moderate
Terrain: mainly tracks, one rocky path early in the walk

BRIEF DESCRIPTION: This walk is relatively easy to follow, and you are treated to good views up and down the two valleys of the Guadiaro and Genal rivers. A chance to stroll round two of the prettier villages of the Genal valley

HOW TO GET THERE: Benadalid is on the A369 Gaucin to Ronda road. Park on the main road by the street leading down to the cemetery which is in the castle below the main road.

THE WALK: facing the castle/cemetery, take the concrete track to the right going downhill and go immediately left when it splits (MAP 1) and follow the left side of the valley. There are large white paint blobs marking the first part of the walk and also the red logo of the Genal 365 route. At the first junction (MAP 2) turn right and, after a zigzag, continue in the same direction until you reach the stream on your right (MAP 3). Cross over and take a recently excavated earth track on the other side of the stream which soon rises up into the woods. This rough track then reduces to a small path after 200 metres. Stay on this path for 1.5 kilometres, until you reach a ridge with a pylon. Drop down the other side and turn left on to a rough track, (MAP 4) which winds in and out of a gully and then passes a ruin. There are no more white paint blobs from now on. Beyond the ruin, cross a shallow gully to climb onto a ridge and veer left by a footpath sign (MAP 5) to follow a track up the ridge which levels out and crosses a deeper gully to arrive below a farm. At a junction turn left up the slope

(MAP 6) and follow this track as it passes round the side of a hill along a steep sided valley and one kilometre from the last junction, passes through a metal gate. Continue on the same track as it soon starts to zigzag up the hillside

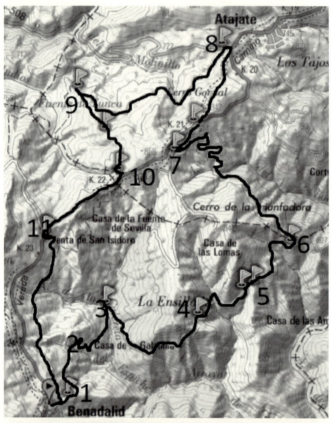

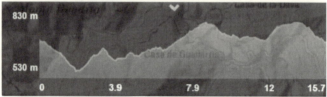

ahead towards the main road. Ignore one right turn one kilometre from the gate and when you reach a T junction, turn right to join the GR 141. (MAP 7) Cross over the road ahead and continue on the GR141 as far as the outskirts of Atajate where it meets the road again. To your left and opposite a venta which faces you, there is a turn off the main road marked Jimera de Libar. (if you wish to visit the pretty village of Atajate, then just cross over the main road and go down a concrete path into the village). Go down here (Jimera road) for 50 metres and turn left down a well-maintained track (MAP 8). Go for almost 2.5 kilometres (40 - 45 minutes). Reach a ridge and just before the track descends round to the left, take a grassy track up the slope to the left (MAP 9) which soon follows a fence on your left. After 10 minutes fork right along a wide grassy track and this meets a gravel track where you turn left.

At the top where the track meets the main road via a padlocked gate, just go left up a narrow path for 30 metres and exit where the fence has been broken down (MAP 10). Turn right and follow the road for about 500 metres (on the right you can walk behind the barrier, which is the GR141 footpath. 50 metres past a track to the right and a ruin on the left, in a break in the barrier, locate the red and white markers of the GR 141 which lead you off the road down a steep path to the left (MAP 11). This becomes a rocky path which follows the contour line below and parallel to the road above all the way to Benadalid. You will emerge with the castle/cemetery to your left. Your car is up to the right.

https://www.wikiloc.com/hiking-trails/benadalid-to-atajate-via-the-bodega-penoncillo-return-via-el-sotillo-walk-116-from-book-5-special-w-32657272

WALK 117   BENADALID - THE DORSAL

Time: 4 hours (10.5 Kilometres)

Difficulty: Hard due to lack of paths

Terrain: rocky path, some track, open rocky terrain

BRIEF DESCRIPTION: the Dorsal is the rocky spine of the ridge running above Benadalid. The route encompasses a section of the GR 141 before climbing very steeply up to the ridge and then traversing to the Col de Benaladid. Use of wikilocs is recommended.

HOW TO GET THERE: on the A369 Ronda to Gaucin road park by the bus shelter by a house at the junction of the road to Benalauria.

THE WALK: take the signposted path opposite the bus shelter going up the slope and then turn right and follow signs for the GR141 which runs parallel to the road towards Benadalid. Pass a radio mast and then after a metal gate turn sharp right down a track to the road. (MAP 1) Cross over and turn left and after 200 metres turn right down a street that leads to the cemetery housed in the former castle. Before you reach the cemetery turn left and follow this track (GR 141) for 2.5 kilometres. (MAP 2)

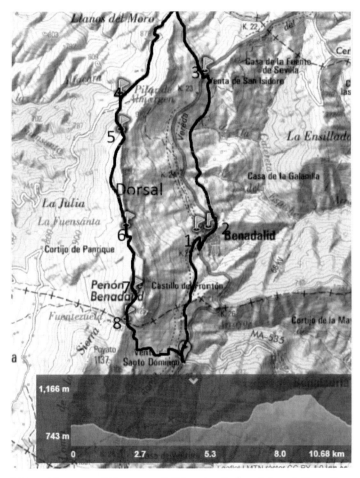

https://www.wikiloc.com/hiking-trails/walk-book-5-walk-117-beadalid-el-dorsal-46371818

After a barbecue area it reduces to a path and it is well signposted when it later reaches a fork. Keep left. You remain below the road until just before a ruin where you veer sharp left to join the road above (MAP 3). Turn right and opposite the ruin take the track opposite. Remain on this track for 2.5 kilometres as it meanders round the back of the Dorsal, passes a sheep farm and reaches a gate.

Pass through the gate and immediately go left off the track at an angle of 30 degrees up a wide grassy path heading due south (MAP 4). This soon peters out and you now enter pine trees and keep to the right of a clifflike promontory to locate a very steep gully. There is no defined route, but there are occasional animal paths zigzagging upwards. Head for the ridge above and you will reach a fence. (MAP 5)

Turn right and follow a faint path which roughly keeps between the thick broom bushes to the right and the rough rock face to the left. Your heading is south keeping roughly 100 metres below the top of the ridge. After 1000 metres from the fence you will join a track zigzagging up from below but it will be visible well beforehand. Dont be tempted to drop down to the track too soon. It is better to maintain height and actually follow the ridge as you approach the track, rounding a rocky outcrop just before you turn left up the track. (MAP 6)

The track peters out after a further 1000 metres (MAP 7). At this point you can turn left and go to the edge to take in the impressive views towards the Sierra de las Nieves. The route actually turns right to follow a rocky path well-marked with cairns down the slope through woods to meet a concrete track (MAP 8), where you turn left to rejoin your car a kilometre further down.

WALK 118   ALGATOCIN – VENTA SAN JUAN TO BENARRABA VIA THE TRAIL DE BICI AND RETURN VIA LLANOS DEL REY AND THE GR 249

Time: 5 hours including a stroll round Benarraba (14 Kilometres)

Difficulty: Easy

Terrain: a couple of very narrow rough paths but mainly on tracks. Streets if you take the tour of Benarraba.

BRIEF DESCRIPTION: this walk incorporates the best the area has to offer, part of the bici trail, the village of Benarraba, the best part of the Llanos del Rey path and the now rebuilt GR249 between La Escribana and Venta San Juan. With a great summer swimming spot just where the Genal has been dammed.

HOW TO GET THERE: From A369 Gaucin to Ronda road turn off at Algatocin signposted Genalguacil and Jubrique. When you reach the river Genal, park at the Venta San Juan.

https://es.wikiloc.com/rutas-senderismo/walk-118-book-5-walks-in-s-andalucia-venta-san-juan-benarraba-return-via-llanos-del-rey-and-gr249-38115794

THE WALK: Walk back across the bridge and then leave a campsite on your left. At the end of the campsite fence, take a track to the left (MAP 1). Then veer right and walk 500 metres up the track following the stream and crossing it via a ford and passing through a gate. Then leave the track to take a small path to the left marked by an uprooted sign indicating the end of the trail de bici. This path initially follows a streambed (usually dry) (MAP2) through thick

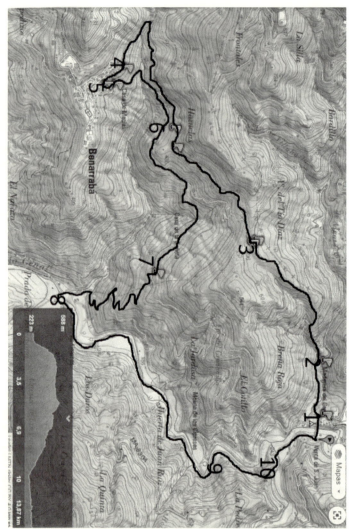

undergrowth and then leaves the streambed and climbs up steeply to the right. Follow the path which is in fact and rather unbelievably a mountain bike trail coming down

From Algatocin so take care in case a biker comes downhill. The path eventually emerges 600 metres later onto a wider track which continues to climb. After a further 600 metres take the right hand fork and then at the next junction turn left downhill to join a major track at a junction (MAP 3). Turn right and follow this track ignoring all turn offs for just under 3 kilometres when you reach the outskirts of Benarraba (MAP 4).

DO take the opportunity of a stroll round this attractive village. See end of this description for map and route for village tour. Bear in mind you need to end up 200 metres down the first street to the left as you enter the village where the path known as the Llanos del Rey starts; There is a panel board here and the path turns left off this street and heads down the slope past a fuente, (water not drinkable).
(the wikiloc track takes the left-hand street which passes by the townhall and then takes the first narrow alleyway to the right to reach a beautifully decorated house called Casa de Cabildo (MAP 5) in a small square with a waterspout opposite a shop. It then bears left down past the church, then right down the side of the church and passes round the lower part of the village to reach the start of the Llanos del Rey path on the right just past a panel board). After 200 metres, cross a stream and continue along the other side of the valley on a very narrow path, eventually widening to a track. Very soon after joining this track take a small path signposted Llanos del Rey to the right down the slope. (MAP 6) Follow this path, taking care as the rain of 2018 has caused some damage with the odd fallen tree and very narrow sections. At the end of the path, drop

steeply down to reach a track where you turn left. After 400 metres you arrive at a track (MAP 7). Turn right, now leaving the green and white flashes of the Llanos del Rey path and zigzag down the hill, eventually through metal gates to reach a track which crosses the River Genal on a low concrete bridge. In the summer the river is dammed just below and with picnic tables on the other side, makes a perfect place for a break and a swim (MAP 8). Just over the bridge take the first path to the left by a cluster of signs and after 50 metres continue to follow the bank of the river at a junction where one branch of the GR249 goes right uphill to Genalguacil. In 2019 there is a sign saying the path is temporally closed but in June 2019 I was able to traverse the next section with ease as substantial repair work has been completed following the devastation by the flood water in October 2018.

The new path has been well used and is easy to follow. After 200 metres you reach the first of the metal walkways. A new path has been cut which climbs high to the right and descends to the walkway. Care is needed just past the metal section where you follow a water channel where in one part you have to edge along a log. This is the only tricky section and can be avoided by just walking up the river-bed and rejoining the right hand bank just beyond the water channel. From now on it is just a question of following the path up the side of the river, transitting the metal walkways as they occur. After 30 minutes you turn left onto a track which passes along the side of a finca (MAP 9). At the gate take the path to the left of the fence. This path now takes you further upstream: when it reaches a tributary, veer left and after 50 metres cross over on a brand new wooden slatted bridge (MAP 10).

On the other side you follow the camp site fence on your right and when you reach a building turn sharp right to climb steeply up a bank behind the building to reach a metalled road which leads into the campsite. Turn left and reach Venta San Juan where at the weekends or in summer there are good meals on offer and the drinks are most refreshing.

MAP FOR TOUR OF BENARRABA

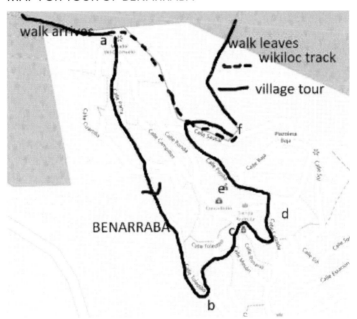

By mirador (MAP a) fork right along Calle Parra, which turns into Calle Toledillo. At (MAP b) turn sharp left down a narrow alley to reach Plazoleta del Cabilde where there is an interesting wall decoration. (MAP c) Head down to Calle Calzada and then to the church (MAP d) Go left along Calle Posito to pass by the Ayuntamiento then take the next right to join Calle Saucel and then reach point f to resume the walk by the panel board for the Sendero Llanos del Rey.

WALK 119 ALGATOCIN TO VENTA-SAN-JUAN- RETURN VIA GR 249 AND LLANOS-DEL-REY

Time: 5 hours (16 kilometres)
Difficulty: moderate
Terrain: rocky paths and some tracks

BRIEF DESCRIPTION: a challenging walk in the picturesque valley of the Genal, incorporating the stunning riverside path called La Pasarela. Nearly 800 metres of height gain.

HOW TO GET THERE. Algatocin is on the A369 Ronda to Gaucin. Park in the main street, the road to Genalguacil

THE WALK: Carry on down the same road past a shop Ferrgenal Ferreteria and take a steep track to the right about 400 metres past the Ferreteria (ironmongers). This joins the road. Turn right and go 100 metres and take the wide path to the left, which cuts off a bend in the road. Turn left at the road, go a further 100 metres and take a track to the right. Go 100 metres and take the left fork. (MAP 1) This track rejoins the road 800 metres later, then leaves on a path to the right. When you next reach the road, cross straight over and take the path opposite. The next time you reach the road go a few metres to the left and take the track to the right which leads to a padlocked gate. (MAP 2). Take a small path to the left of the gate running parallel to the track. It rejoins the track and on a sharp right-hand bend take a rough path (MAP 3) to the left, which winds down the hill and reaches the road below. Turn right, follow the bend to the left, and then turn right through a wire and post gate. Follow a steep path dropping down the slope, which reaches a track below. Turn left and reach the road after 100 metres. Turn right and follow the road as far as the Venta San Juan the other side of the bridge over the river Genal. Turn right at the car park and follow a track leading to the gates of a campsite. (MAP 4) Take a path to the right which leads to the river and then follows it down stream. You are on the GR 249/141. Pass by a finca and join a track. The track soon leaves the river while you veer right onto a metal walkway above the river (MAP 5). There are more walkways further on and you now continue for a further 2 kilometres to reach a recreation/picnic area where there is a concrete bridge across the river (MAP 6). Cross the bridge and turn right. Follow the track uphill through a gate after 400 metres. At just under 2 kilometres from the river turn left after a right-hand bend, along a track marked by green and white markers. This is a local path called the Llanos del Rey. (MAP 7) After 600 metres, on a left-hand bend, take a small path up to the right (MAP 8) which now snakes around the side of the hill to reach a wider path 1200 metres later. Turn right (MAP 9) and go 100 metres or so to reach a driveable track. Turn right and go 800 metres to then take a very steep path up to the left through trees (MAP 10). Just before a fence turn left onto a well-used path still climbing alongside the fence. (If you don´t fancy this very steep path go a further 100 metres along the track and turn left up a side track and then immediately left again up a well-used path alongside a fence) Pass through a gate, the path now a track, and then leave two farms on the right.

Then turn right at a junction where there is a pylon (MAP 11) and now on the PR239 path from Benarraba to Algatocin, continue uphill to another junction where again you turn right to leave the PR. You are on a downhill section, but after an attractive house alongside the track, (MAP 12) you gradually start climbing now on a rocky path with Algatocin looming above you. The path expands to become a concrete track, to reach the street where your car is parked and where you started the walk.

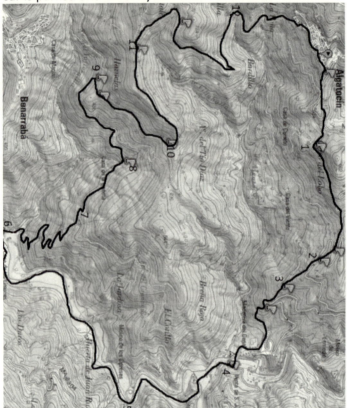

https://www.wikiloc.com/hiking-trails/walk-book-5-walk-119-algatocin-to-venta-san-juan-return-via-la-escribana-46277312

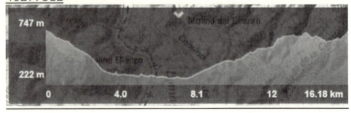

WALK 120 ALGATOCIN – TOWARDS BENARRABA AND RETURN VIA LOS GUINDALES, ALGATOCIN, INSTITUTO AND LAS PILAS

Time: 4 hours (15 Kilometres)
Difficulty: easy
Terrain: mostly tracks one steep rocky path ascending

BRIEF DESCRIPTION: A most enjoyable walk spent initially in the Genal valley, and then returning along the high ridge above Algatocin with views of both the Genal and Guadiaro valleys and beyond.

HOW TO GET THERE: Take the A369 Ronda to Gaucin road and 2 kilometres south of Algatocin park at the start of the Bici de Montana trail. It is 100 metres south of the entrance to a Mirador.

THE WALK: take the Bici trail (watch out for cyclists at weekends) downhill past a couple of fincas and after 1 kilometre arrive at a T junction. (MAP 1) The bici trail turns left and you turn right to briefly follow the PR238 (yellow and white bands) in the direction of Benarraba just below you.

You then meet another T junction. The PR continues to the right while you turn left to join a local route known as the Llanos del Rey (MAP 2). This runs along the contour line along a good track for just over 2 kilometres. 100 metres past a turn off to the right, turn sharp left (MAP 3) and 100 metres later veer left again up a rough track, which is the bici trail but you are now following it in reverse! It soon becomes a steep rocky path, (one wonders how the cyclists manage to descend without coming off!) and then levels out to pass a farm, now a track again.

The track reaches a junction by a pylon. (MAP 4) Turn right and continue up the hill. At the next junction turn right (MAP 5) and this track goes downhill now approaching Algatocin, which comes into view round the next corner. Keep left on a corner with a side turning to the right and as you approach a house alongside the track ignore a left turn going up the slope to a wooden house.

MAP FOR FIRST AND LAST PART OF THE WALK

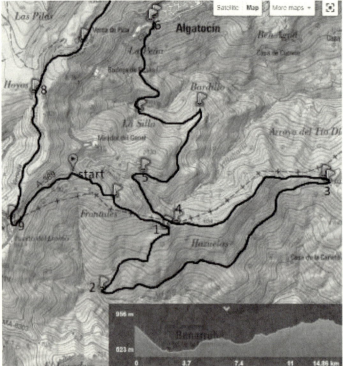

105

Pass by the house and continue round the side of the hill the track reducing to a path which now climbs the hill to enter Algatocin, up a concrete track. Turn left when you

MAP FOR MIDDLE PART OF WALK

reach the road and then turn right into the square by a bar (MAP 6). Pass through the right-hand side of the square along Avenida Andalucia and then Calle Perez Jimenez. At the end veer left and slightly downhill towards a block of flats. As the concrete street bends right behind the flats, a panel board marks the start of a walk which goes to the Fuente Las Pilas, the route you will now follow.

The track leaves the village on a contour line but then climbs gradually up towards the main road passing through the car park of the Secondary School to your right. At the road turn left and take the track up the hill off to the right a few metres on. (MAP 7) Pass the new cemetery and after 2.5 kilometres you will reach the Fuente de las Pilas, which has good drinking water. Continue climbing the hill and just over the top, at a junction of tracks veer left by a signpost indicating Puerto del Espino 1200 metres away (MAP 8).

This path follows the ridge southwards and crosses over towards the main road below. Drop down to the road, turn left (MAP 9) and your car is 300 metres away.

https://www.wikiloc.com/hiking-trails/walk-120-from-book-special-walks-algatocin-to-benarraba-and-return-via-los-guindales-algatocin-inst-34132497

WALK 121 JUBRIQUE - VENTA SAN JUAN – GR 141 – ERMITA SANTA CRUZ

Time: 4 hours (12 kilometres)
Difficulty: moderate
Terrain: paths track and road

BRIEF DESCRIPTION: a delightful walk shown to me by Chris Thorogate a long term resident of Jubrique, and a fount of local knowledge. Some steep ascents rewarded by fine views up and down the Genal valley.

HOW TO GET THERE: from the A369 Gaucin to Ronda road take the MA 8305 from Algatocin to Jubrique. Venta de San Juan is just over the bridge over the River Genal.

THE WALK: Go behind the Venta and take the road which leads to a campsite. Take the path to the right of the gates, This is the GR 249/141 which you follow for the first part of the walk. You then drop down towards the river passing by a cottage and the perimeter fence of the camping ground. Then cross a side stream on a new bridge and the path generally follows the banks of the Genal river after briefly leaving the river. After 15 minutes you join a track coming from a finca (MAP 1) and you now follow it up the side of the valley to a road above.

Turn right (MAP 2) and after 400 metres turn left onto a steep track which passes through gates (MAP 3). If padlocked then keep left in the gully and then rejoin the track. The track winds up the hill. After 500 metres pass by a cottage and immediately turn left at a junction, (MAP 4), along a track which starts on the level then starts descending.

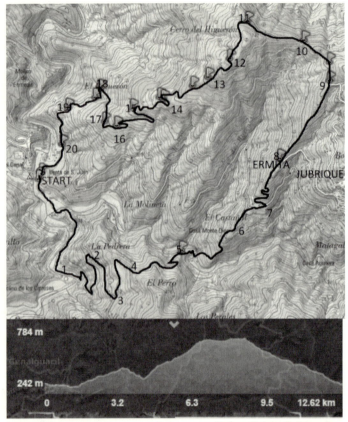

https://www.wikiloc.com/hiking-trails/walk-book-5-walk-121-venta-s-juan-ermita-jubrique-from-special-walks-in-s-andalucia-45616377

After 700 metres, on a right-hand bend take a path to the left (MAP 5), which follows a narrow ridge down to the stream below. Cross over and take a path which clmbs steeply the other side. 700 metres from the bottom, turn right on to a gravel track (MAP 6) which meets a road after 300 metres.

Turn right and at a junction 200 metres further on turn left signposted Farajan and Ermita Santa Cruz (MAP 7). Climb for 500 metres and the Ermita is on your right.

Opposite the Ermita, take a small path uphill to the right of a track and to the left of metal gates (MAP 8). The path leads up the hill for one kilometre to the Farajan road (MAP 9). Turn left, go 200 metres and turn left down a gravel track signposted to Benalauria on the PR 291. After 200 metres take the middle of 3 tracks with a yellow and white cross (MAP 10). 300 metres later take a left fork through gates (MAP 11). After 500 metres, edge right down a rough track passing over 2 fallen trees (MAP 12).

Turn right down a steep path after 300 metres (MAP 13). 200 metres later, cross over a track, then another 200 metres later turn right onto a track. Go 200 metres and turn right on to another track. After 100 metres take a steep path to the left, (MAP 14) which descends to a track below, following a fence on your left. Turn left and after a couple of bends take the left fork where the track splits. (MAP 15) Go downhill for 800 metres and on a left hand bend take a track to the right (MAP 16). After 100 metres take a path to the right of a wooden slatted gate (MAP 17). Go through two wire gates, pass a stone hut and drop down the side of the hill on a faint path. Cross over a steep gully and then edge down the slope to a wider path below. (MAP 18) Turn left, cross back over the gully and take the right-hand path at a fork. Follow this for about 300 metres and then pass through a bedstead gate in a fence to your left.

A rough path takes you down to a track, where you turn left, downhill to a road (MAP 19). Turn right to return to the Venta San Juan where your car is parked.

WALK 122 TO GENALGUACIL ON GR 249 AND RETURN VIA CAMINO DE LOS BAÑOS DEL DUQUE

Time: 4 hours (13.5 kilometres)
Difficulty: Moderate
Terrain: paths and track, mostly on GR 249

BRIEF DESCRIPTION: an enchanting walk, using the GR249, a long-distance footpath which takes you up to and through Genalguacil, an attractive village perched above the Genal valley adorned with interesting street art. You continue up the Almarchal valley crossing over the river and returning on well-made tracks with great views the whole way round.

HOW TO GET THERE: drive to Benarraba from the A369 Ronda to Gaucin road and as you arrive in the village by Bar Guayacan turn sharp right by a cluster of footpath signs. Go down this small road to the bottom of the valley ignoring one turn to the right and park in the large flat area on the other side of the river Genal, crossing on a concrete bridge.

THE WALK: return to the bridge and take the path marked with a way post to the right just before the bridge. Skirt round the side of a house and turn right up a steep path which is the GR249 heading to Genalguacil. Cross over two tracks (MAP 1) and continue climbing the ridge making sure at (MAP 2) you keep right on the path which drops down a bank. Pass a multi-use sports pitch on your left and reach the road (MAP 3). Turn right and follow the road into the village of Genalguacil. Take the main street (marked occasionally with plaques on the ground displaying the GR249 logo) through the village passing the Town Hall on your right towards the far end. At the church you can turn right into a square with great views at the far end.

https://www.wikiloc.com/hiking-trails/walk120-to-genalguacil-on-gr-249-and-return-via-camino-de-los-banos-del-duque-33887011

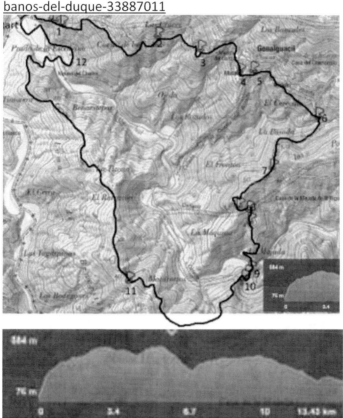

Return to the church and just beyond (MAP 4) take the right hand of two streets which goes steeply downhill to a dead end.

This is the continuation of the GR 249 and at the bottom take a small path up a bank to the left marked with a red and white marker post. (MAP 5) This path climbs up to a track where you turn right and head downhill. 100 metres before reaching a gate turn left down a small path indicated by a waymark. (MAP 6) This path crosses a stream and wends its way round the side of the valley towards a road. At one stage a fallen olive tree has blocked the path. Edge round the bottom and a marker post will indicate your route up the bank to rejoin the path.

At the road turn right and go 100 metres to a left-hand bend. Here, indicated by a finger post, turn right along the GR249 towards Casares (MAP 7). You now follow the GR along the ridge on a track, then down the hill to the left after a zigzag. Look out for an overgrown track off to the right; there is no waymark but if you overshoot there is a post with an X on it indicating this is not the way (MAP 8). Turn right down the overgrown track and a waymark will confirm you are on the correct route after a few metres. The track reduces to a rocky path and you descend into the picturesque valley of the Almarchal. After passing a goat farm on the right, cross the river and edge right to climb the recently devastated bank to join a track. (A severe rainstorm in 2018 caused flooding and the waters have destroyed the banks of the river and washed away many trees and bushes)

Go just a few metres and then turn sharp right up a very steep path marked by a way post (MAP 9). Climb steeply for 200 metres and reach a track. (MAP 10) Turn right and follow the track for just over 2 kilometres gradually climbing the side of the valley to reach a ridge. When you reach a junction, the GR249 turns left while you turn right downhill where there is a way post with a yellow and white band. (MAP 11)

Stay on this track all the way down this ridge ignoring all side turnings until you reach the river Almarchal at the bottom just over 3 kilometres later. Cross the river and turn left at the junction 100 metres up the slope (MAP 12), to rejoin your car 500 metres down the track.

WALK 123   CASARES – CRESTELLINA

Time / distance: 5 hours including ascent of Crestellina / 12 Kilometres (shorter alternative 4 hours – see text)
Difficulty: hard due to ascent of Crestellina
Terrain: paths, tracks and rough mountainside on Crestellina

BRIEF DESCRIPTION: A varied walk, taking in the Crestellina mountain, then passing briefly through a private estate on a right of way, then along the edge of a mountainside urbanisation, and finally through the picturesque village of Casares and across a valley to return to the start. (There is a shorter option avoiding the private estate -see text).

HOW TO GET THERE.   From the coast take the A377 to Casares, from inland take the A377 from Gaucin and then MA 528 left to Casares. Before you reach Casares on a left-hand bend there is the tourist office with a car park on the right. Park here.

THE WALK: from the car park turn left, go a few metres along the road then take the first track on the right, then keep left at the next fork. This track goes parallel to the road for about one kilometre and after ignoring two tracks to the right, turn right up the hill at a T junction (MAP 1). Pass a yellow painted house on the left and when the track turns into a farm pass through a wire gate in a fence in front of you (MAP 2). There is a green and white flash. Now take a rough path which starts to climb the mountainside, with green and white flashes marking the route. It is steep and rough in places.

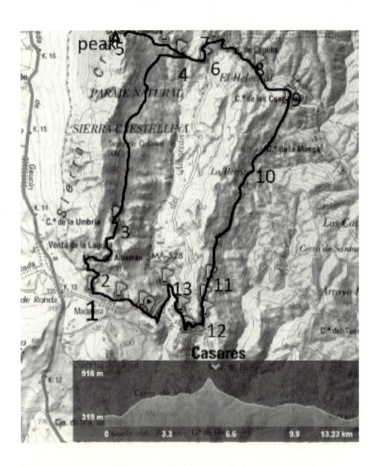

https://www.wikiloc.com/hiking-trails/crestellina-from-casares-tourist-office-return-via-monteduque-and-celina-from-book-50-special-walks-31557002

Eventually you arrive at what was once a cultivated side of the mountain with a couple of springs and small ponds above you. Keep climbing and pass an abandoned shack, amongst terracing 50 metres to your right and you will reach a flatter area. At this point the path is more obvious and together with the green and white flashes you should find your way up to the ridge ahead and down the other side to meet a wider track just above a building in the trees below. (MAP 3) Turn left and follow this track, skirting the side of the Crestellina for the next 2.5 kilometres. When you reach a turning to the left, go up here. (MAP 4)

After 5 minutes ignore one track to the right and soon your track reduces to a path passing through thick gorse and other rough vegetation. At a small clearing there is a cairn ahead indicating the start of the very rough path up the mountain. You now need to follow this path to the left which climbs steeply and is well marked with cairns. It passes alongside some rocky outcrops and heads for the right hand of the two main peaks. The upper part is strewn with many cairns as walkers have marked their own particular route. Arrive at the right-hand edge of the rocky outcrop near a tiny concrete hut which once housed equipment for a radio mast. Then make your way up the outcrop to the summit (MAP 5) and enjoy views across to Africa, Gibraltar and in the opposite direction, the Genal valley and various white villages splattered on the hillsides towards Ronda. Retrace your steps downhill until you reach the junction where you first turned left up the mountain. Turn left and head downhill. After 200 metres pass a sign pointing back up the Crestellina and a track off to the right, and then 200 metres later arrive at a junction of tracks, with footpath signs. (MAP 6)

116

At this point you have a choice: Option A to return direct to the start point if you dont wish to traverse the private Monteduque estate. If you choose this option, then turn right and follow the signs and track to the main road on the outskirts of Casares. Turn right and cross over to follow a very smart pavement along the road back to your car 1 kilometre up the road.

OPTION B: the complete walk: (see map below which shows the right of way if you are stopped) Turn left down a track signposted to Genalguacil on the GR249. After 200 metres you reach a padlocked gate. Drop down to the right and there is a pedestrian gate. Pass through and continue downhill to a junction (MAP 7). Turn right and go downhill for about 500 metres looking for a steep rough track on the right on the other side of a ditch. (MAP 8) Go up here, following a fence until you join a track coming up from the left. Turn right and up the slope there is a gate leading to a track the other side. (MAP 9)

MAP SHOWING RIGHT OF WAY (VEREDA)

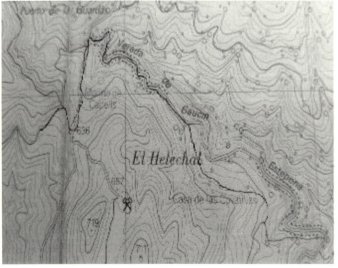

Follow this track, forking right up a steep concrete track past a finca with a barking dog. When you come to a turning up to the right with a sign saying to La Manga go up here (MAP 10) and after 100 metres just before entrance gates go left down a path which then follows the contour line for several hundred metres until it joins a concrete track. Turn right and continue uphill and over the ridge. On the other side the track starts descending and reaches a junction of tracks. (MAP 11) At this point you leave the track into bushes on your right down a narrow path descending into a gully. You then join a track coming from your right which you effectively cross over and continue down the same gully on the path while the track goes up the slope to your left.

When you reach the road below, turn right (MAP 12). Pass a couple of bars and then after rounding the corner to the right, take a flight of steps by a mirador which leads down to the main part of the village. When you reach the main square turn right down Calle Carrera and when the street forks, take the left-hand street (Camino Gaucin) downhill which meanders down to cross a mediaeval bridge (MAP 13) and then turns left to climb the hill up to the tourist office. Your car is parked on the other side.

WALK 124   CASARES/MANILVA - RIO MANILVA AND ROMAN BATHS

Time: 4 hours including a swim in the sulphur baths (10 kilometres) (add 30 minutes for the via ferrata)
Difficulty: moderate
Terrain: rough paths, track and short stretch of road.

BRIEF DESCRIPTION: a walk taking in a spectacular gorge, the Canuto, the river Manilva, "roman" baths and an optional diversion to try an easy via ferrata.

HOW TO GET THERE: from Manilva/ San Luis de Sabinillas take the A377 direction Gaucin or from Gaucin the same road. Between Kilometre 8 and 9 on the right from the coast (left from Gaucin) there is a track leading to piles of rocks. It is opposite the entrance to the maintenance building of the wind turbines. Park down this track (there is a large flat area 50 metres down)

THE WALK: 50 metres down from the road take the left hand track down the hill. At the next fork go right (MAP 1), and then straight on at the next fork. 150 metres from the last fork, where the track goes sharp right go straight on down a rough grassy track where there is a rather broken-down wire and post gate 50 metres down. (MAP 2) Then veer right downhill down a path through an open field and head towards a building, a disused mill with an aquaduct leading in behind. Go to the right, cross a stream to the left of three poplar trees and locate a path going into the bushes and towards a cliff where there is a rough path behind a wooden fence. (MAP 3)

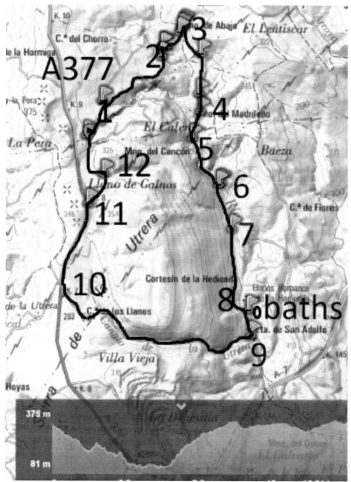

https://www.wikiloc.com/walking-trails/rio-manilva-and-the-roman-baths-return-via-canuto-walk-124-from-book-5-31351333

(This wikiloc track has an extra 5 Kilometres from the end of the walk to the Venta Laguna on the A377 direction Gaucin)

Turn right and follow this path below the cliff until it becomes a wider track now climbing the slope to the left. Pass through one wire and post gate and near the top merge with a track from the left through a wire and post gate. Head down the ridge and you will approach a farm with a house to the right. (MAP 4)

Turn left at the next junction and drop down the hill to a large metal gate at the bottom which leads to an equestrian centre (this is a public right of way from Casares to Manilva). Follow the well- maintained gravel track through this property and when you reach the stream go straight on to the left of a derelict building on a path which leads through a metal gate and then along the side of a spectacular gorge (MAP 5), with the stream below you on your right. The path is steep in places but eventually drops down to the streambed. The path the other side is blocked by a fallen tree but just go 10 metres upstream to cross over and pick up the path. (MAP 6)(*If you wish to try the via ferrata you should follow the stream up for 200 metres and you will find a set of chains and foot rests set in the rockface. It will lead up first on the left side of the stream then up a cliff on the opposite side back to the path you were on earlier*)

You now follow the stream on the right-hand side, but after 200 metres you are obliged to cross back over as you approach the boundary fence of a property. There are yellow and white flashes to mark the route.

Once past the boundary fence cross back over on a path through thick bushes which meets a track by the entrance gate to the property (MAP 7). Turn left and follow this track for just over a kilometre when you pass an entrance gate to your left. 100 metres further on there are steps down to the left which lead to the Roman Baths. (Baños de Hedionda) They are sulphurous and it is possible to bathe there. (MAP 8)

Return to the track and continue past a chapel on your left and then just after the track crosses a streambed and bends left, take a path to the right which leads to the spectacular gorge of the Canuto (MAP 9). This path (marked as a Senda Local with green and white flashes) climbs up on large slabs through the gorge to emerge by a derelict concrete water reservoir. Continue up the hill, the path becomes a track and then passes through a farm, turning right, then left to reach the road (MAP 10). Turn right here and go 800 metres until you pass a 60 KPH sign then 100 metres later turn right off the road through a wire and post gate (MAP 11) onto a grassy path which soon bends to the left downhill. (If this gate is padlocked then continue along the road for 200 metres and turn right to reach your car) At the bottom veer left by a cairn (MAP 12) and follow a rough path through bushes and then along the streambed before veering right up the slope past the piles of rocks to where your car is parked.

WALK 125   CASARES TO LACIPO

Time: 4 hours (13 Kilometres)
Difficulty: moderate
Terrain: tracks and rough paths

BRIEF DESCRIPTION: a historically themed walk including a medieval bridge, roman remains, a moorish village, and a Spanish Civil War memorial. It is also an attractive walk with views up and down the Genal valley.

HOW TO GET THERE: From the A377 Manilva to Gaucin road, turn off towards Casares on the MA528. Go l kilometre and park at the Tourist Information Office car park on the right.

THE WALK: from the car park face the tourist office and take the track to the left which heads down the hill with Casares to your right across the valley. At the bottom cross an old stone bridge (puente medieval) and veer right up a concrete track (Camino de Gaucin) towards the village. (MAP 1) Veer right at a junction and then right again where you join the main street (Calle Carrera) leading to the square. Cross the square (to visit upper town go straight on up Calle Villa) and go slightly left by a sign on the wall indicating despacho de Pan and then go right down a narrow street (MAP 2) (Calle de Juan Ceron) which leads downhill and out of the village heading south. As you reach a hill ahead fork right down a grassy track (MAP 3) and skirt round the side down to a junction. Turn right and go a few metres to visit the War Memorial (MAP 4). Retrace your steps, turning left back up the hill for 300 metres to turn left down a rocky path marked with green and white stripes (MAP 5). Proceed to the bottom of the gully and cross the

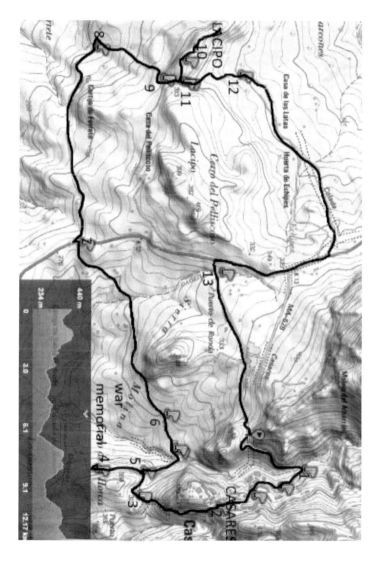

https://www.wikiloc.com/hiking-trails/casares-lacipo-from-walk-book-special-walks-in-southern-andalucia-34821757 streambed. Go 200 metres and cross over a track and continue on the other side, marked with green and white stripes. At the next track (MAP 6), go left and follow the track all the way to the road passing various fincas. Turn left at the road, go 50 metres and turn right down a country lane crossing a cattle grid (MAP 7).

After passing a farm on your right take the next track to the right up open ground where cattle may be grazing (MAP 8). Go 500 metres up the hill and after a right-hand bend turn left by a fence and pass through a gate (MAP 9) into a wooded area climbing more steeply up a stony path. As you reach a ridge veer left and continue up the path and you will reach a flatter area with the vestiges of the roman site of Lacipo. A prominent section of wall is to your left (MAP 10).

You can continue along the ridge to visit the rest of the site but it needs some imagination to work out how the roman town was laid out. Return to MAP 11 and then turn left to follow a faint path between gorse bushes which meanders down the hill to a wire gate in a fence to a track just beyond a shallow pond (MAP 12). Turn right follow a well-maintained gravel track all the way up to the road.

Turn right, pass the turn-off to Casares and sfter a further 500 metres, turn left down a track which leads down to metal gates (MAP 13). As you reach the gates go left and pick up a cobbled path running along a fence and then passing a few fincas to your left. It then passes below an industrial building to run parallel to the road above, to finally climb steeply up to the car park where you left your car.

WALK 126 GRAZALEMA - GAIDOVAR AND MONTE CERRO COROS

Time: 5 hours (13 Kilometres)
Difficulty; medium
Terrain: rough paths, section of quiet road

BRIEF DESCRIPTION: a dramatic walk passing by a pretty reservoir then dropping down to Gaidovar to pick up a scenic path leading up to Monte Cerro Coros. Return via Puerto de Poloma.

HOW TO GET THERE: Grazalema is on the A 372. Park at the top of the village on Calle Nueva.

THE WALK: continue down the street and on the first corner where it turns right go left up a path and then after a few metres, turn right along a rough path into bushes to the Guadalete stream which you cross. The path then wends its way to the right round the side of the hill towards a dam rising above you. There is the remains of a water pipe embedded along the path.

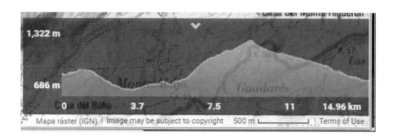

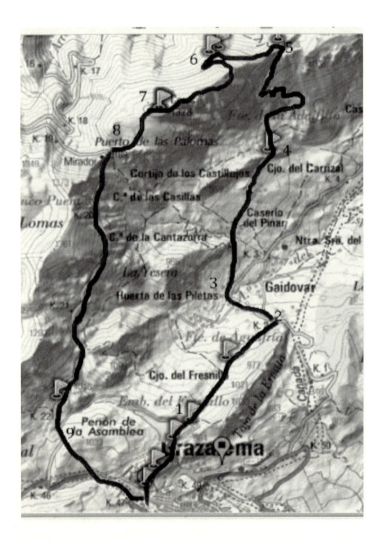

https://www.wikiloc.com/hiking-trails/grazalema-circular-via-monte-cerro-coros-23911046
courtesy Matthew Wolfman

Just below the dam, cross the stream bed and either climb the stairs leading up the side of the dam or take the path. At the top turn right on to a track. Go a few metres and as the track curves round the side of the reservoir to the left, you leave the track to the right on a rough path (MAP 1), first crossing over a gully and then heading down the left-hand side, crossing over a couple of times. You keep a fence/wall on your left the whole way down until you reach a road (MAP 2).

Turn left and after a few metres take a rough track then path running parallel and to the right of the road. After 200 metres you emerge back on the road and as it bends to the right take a track to the left (MAP 3), initially running parallel to the road, then heading towards the steep mountainside. Ignore one turn to the left then pass close by a farm on your left, through a gate to enter wilder countryside.

The track peters out in a grassy area and you continue on a rough path in the same direction, north, through a fence. 200 metres later the path splits (MAP 4). Go left up the slope and follow this path all the way up the steep side of the mountain. First, negotiate a large landslide, then reach woods and a fence where you turn left to climb steeply via zigzags and a wire and post gate 200 metres before you arrive at the ridge (MAP 5).

Here you pass through a gap in a rather broken-down fence and turn immediately left up the fence to join a rough path heading right round the side of the hill on the contour line. Keep left when the path splits after 200 metres.

Now the path climbs steeply and 500 metres later there is another junction (MAP 6). Turn left to follow cairns back up to the ridge and along to the summit of Monte Cerro Los Coros where there is a trig point (MAP 7). Then drop down on the path to the road below as it passes through the Puerto de la Paloma where there is a car park and mirador (MAP 8).

Turn left and follow this very quiet road for nearly three kilometres, passing a carpark on the right and gated track on the left. 100 metres later leave the track on a path to the left entering woods. 400 metres later, after crossing a track, rejoin the road, turning left to return to the village. Your car will be down the first street on the left.

View of the Zahara reservoir from the top of Cerro Los Coros

WALK 127 MONTEJAQUE/GRAZALEMA - CAMPOBUCHE ALAMO WALK

Time: 5 hours / 15 kilometres
Difficulty: medium
Terrain: track and paths. open fields

BRIEF DESCRIPTION: a mainly flat walk between Montejaque and Grazalema along ancient rights of way including the rio Guadares.

HOW TO GET THERE. From Montejaque, take the MA 8403 and after 100 m take the first track to the left. Go 5 K passing close by a farm after 4 K and then a turn off over a bridge. 1 K later park where the track forks. The wikiloc track starts here. From Grazalema take the A372 direction Ronda. At the junction of the road to Villalengua bear left and turn right by a venta up a track and drive 2 kilometres to park where the track crosses a stream.

THE WALK: (from Grazalema, follow the right bank of the Rio Guadares heading east, until you reach MAP 11 after about 10 minutes.) From Montejaque take the left-hand fork (the right has a chain across) heading uphill and south. Pass through a gate and and 1.2 K from the start (15 minutes) turn left, cross the stream and go through a metal gate on the right just beyond the stream. Follow the left hand side of the stream as near as you can, on rough paths through bushes for 500 m (10 minutes) joining a grassy track which leaves the stream, climbs a little and passes through a gate (MAP 2). Now veer right back down to the stream and cross over at a gap in the bushes. After a few metres veer left up the slope and meet a grassy track where you turn left and follow until it reaches a reaches a fence.

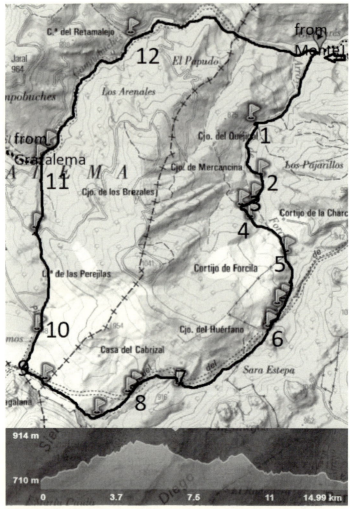

To the left of a wired-up gate, pass through the fence where others have before (MAP 4). Head back down towards the stream, crossing a gully and pick up a path heading southeast following the stream. Pass through a gate at MAP 5. Your objective now is to reach a track running at 90 degrees about 15 minutes further upstream. The best route is to keep close to the stream (the wikiloc track strays to the right from time to time) and after crossing over a track, when you reach a fence in front of you veer right up a gully for 50 metres and find the place where it has been broken down (MAP 6). Climb up the steep bank and turn right onto the track. After 100 metres leave the track through a gate to the left and head south-west leaving a long wall to your left. Pass through a gate, then at a finger post (MAP 7), take the right fork downhill. The path passes through woods then reaches a track at (MAP 8). Turn left, shortly pass through a gate and continue downhill to join a track near a stream. Go through two gates following the stream on your left now heading north west.

As the hill on your left dwindles away you reach a junction (MAP 9). Turn right and follow this track back to the car if you started from Grazalema. Otherwise, at the top of the rise, after 200 metres, leave the track to pass through a small gate to the right (MAP 10). You are aiming north to cross a valley to join a track the other side which leads to a farm. There is no clear path here. Turn right at the track and at the farm pass down the right-hand side heading north on a stony path which leads to a fence. There is way through the fence in the trees on your left. Continue north down an open area into trees towards the bottom of the valley of the Guadares/Campobuche. Pass through a gate at MAP 11 and turn right on to a path which now follows the river on the right-hand side for two kilometres (20 minutes) when you meet a track by a bridge where the river becomes a lake (MAP 12). Turn right and after 30 metres go left to follow the lakeside. After 10 minutes leave the lake on the same path which heads into the woods. After 15 minutes (just over a kilometre, pass through a metal gate to join a wide track which leads to where your car is parked.

WALK 128   GRAZALEMA - RELOJ/SIMANCON CIRCUIT

Time: 4.5 hours (11 kilometres)
Difficulty: hard due to climb and terrain
Terrain: rough paths and open rock face

BRIEF DESCRIPTION: A spectacular walk up to the twin peaks of Simancon and Reloj which overlook the village of Grazalema. The views are in all directions and on a clear day you can see the Atlantic as well as the Mediterranean coast.

HOW TO GET THERE: If driving, Grazalema is on the A372. Park at the west (top) end of the village in a car park adjacent to Camping Tajo Rodrillo.

THE WALK: If staying in Grazalema, start at the town hall. Take the street to the right of Unicaja Bank along Calle Jose Maria Jimenez. Turn left at the top, following Calle Doctor Mateos Gago, then left up Calle Porta, then next right, Calle Nueva past a spring, to arrive at the top of the village. Veer left past the Fromandal cheese factory to arrive at the Grazalema El Bosque road the A372.

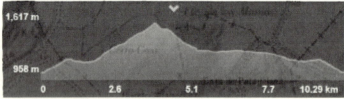

Go a few metres to to the right and there is a car park on the left. Head for a panel board at the back of the car park indicating the Complejo Subbetico, then go left via a green gate to join a rough path the other side. The wikiloc track starts here. You can also leave your car here. (see HOW TO GET THERE)

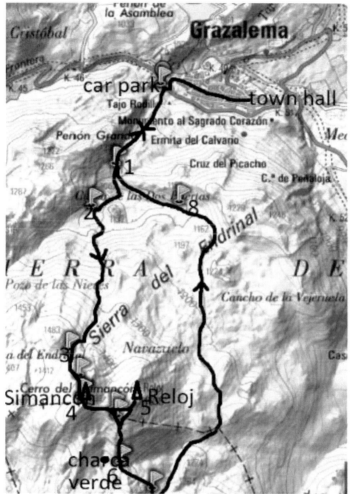

https://www.wikiloc.com/hiking-trails/walk-127-from-book-special-walks-in-s-andalucia-reloj-simancon-34571809

After looping left, pass through a metal gate and climb steeply. You reach the top of this climb, then drop 50 metres down a slope to a signpost. Go straight on down to the valley floor then fork right at a junction (MAP 1).

You now climb up through large rocks. When you reach a flat grassy area take a faint path to the left marked by a cairn (MAP 2). You are now heading south climbing up a wide gully. Just under 2 Kilometres from the last junction you reach a wide plateau with the Simancon mountain looming above you to the left. Leave the path by a large cairn and head left to tackle the open mountain side. (MAP 3) Your direction will be nearer south than southeast as the summit is at the southern end of the ridge above. A large cairn marks the summit at 1569 metres (MAP 4).

From the summit you first locate the second peak of Reloj due east. To reach it head down slightly to the right of the Simancon towards a rocky spine connecting the two peaks. There are a few cairns to guide lower down. Once across the spine veer left when it looks reasonable and head north east to reach the summit (MAP 5). (The wikilocs track continues down to the south as on the day, the wind was dangerously strong!)

Retrace your steps from Reloj and frequent cairns will guide you down the slope heading south towards a saddle with a small pond as a landmark. (Charca Verde) As the path flattens out take a left fork marked by a cairn (MAP 6). You are now heading southeast through jagged rocks and scattered trees. At the next junction keep left and head north with the mass of the Reloj to your left (MAP 7). You remain on this path for at least 3 kilometres on fairly level ground but generally losing height. Pass one path off to the right (MAP 8) and then reach a junction where you passed by earlier in the walk (MAP 1).

Turn right and cross over the ridge to then drop steeply down to the car park and the start of the path.

WALK 129   GRAZALEMA - PINSAPAR

Time: 5.5 hours (17 kilometres) (20 K the full circular) (12 K the short version)
Difficulty: moderate
Terrain: paths and tracks
NB permit needed from park authorities
email: **cv_elbosque@agenciamedioambienteyagua.es**
telephone :   **956 70 97 33** (Centro de visitantes P.N Sierra de Grazalema (El Bosque). You can also collect a permit in Grazalema Tourist Office.

BRIEF DESCRIPTION: A walk in the forest of pinsapo trees - the famous prehistoric pine. Look out for these on the first part of the walk below the Torreon the 1600 m peak on your left. After skirting the mountain side, cross the road to return on picturesque paths and tracks with views down towards Benaocaz.

HOW TO GET THERE: take the A372 from Grazalema direction El Bosque and after 1 kilometre turn right towards Zahara. Go 600 metres and there is a car park on the left. If you dont wish to walk the final 4.5 kilometres then leave a second car at a layby on the left where a track leaves the A372, 2.3 kilometres from Puerto del Boyar. You can further reduce the length of the walk by leaving a second car at the Area Recreativa Llanos del Campo a further 3 kilometres down the road.

THE WALK: starts from the car park, on a path that climbs initially, from 1000 metres to 1275 metres for about 1.5 kilometres, crosses a ridge (MAP 1) and heads along the right-hand side of EL Torreon, occasionally reaching 1300 metres and then descending gradually.   5.8 kilometres

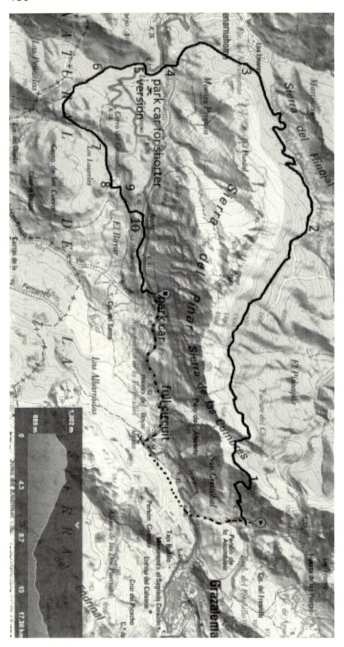

from the start, you join a track from te right, having passed through the pinsapo forest (MAP 2). Almost immediately, turn left on to a path which cuts off a loop of the track and rejoins it after 600 metres. You then go 2.8 kilometres descending and zigzagging with Benaohoma below, and as the track bends to the right take a path to the left (MAP 3). There is a wall with a fence on the corner. You are at 570 metres altitude and about 9 kilometres from the start of the walk.

You climb gently for about a kilometre on a picturesque path ignoring any side paths, and a few metres before you reach the road at 630 metres there is a finger post and a track. To the right there is a gate leading to the road. (MAP 4) Take a path straight across the track, signposted to Area Recreativa and follow a fence to reach a picnic area. Pass through and leave via a gate into a car park. (If you have opted for the short version your car will be here.) Cross the road and go through a gate with a panel board saying sendero Llanos de Berral (MAP 5), on a path leading through trees to a track. Turn left and follow it gently downhill for 600 metres then take a rough track to the left (MAP 6) leading up a grassy slope into trees. It reverts to a path but is easy to follow up a gully between two hills. It gradually reaches a gap in the ridge and edges left and you are now facing the mass of the Torreon mountain.

You next join a more substantial path (MAP 7) where you edge right, and soon you see a small farmstead ahead. Dont go to the farm on the track but continue straight up the hill on the same path to reach a track a hundred metres further on. (MAP 8) Cross straight over and the path cuts a corner of the track which you meet in another hundred metres. Turn left and this track drops down to meet a very well-made track.

Cross straight over and take a rough path up the slope into woods (MAP 9). The road is above, and your aim is to head up towards the road. You reach a fence below the road, easy to climb via a stone wall (MAP 10). Between the fence and the road there is a path and by turning right you can follow it back to your car. Just before you reach your car, you will arrive at a track where you turn left and pass through a gate to reach the road where your car is parked.

 If you dont have a car there, then turn right up the road to walk 4.5 kilometres back to the Pinsapar car park. You pass over the Puerto del Boyar and at the car park on the right just over the pass, you can take a path running down the valley parallel to the road to your left. As it approaches the road again, rejoin the road, turn left then right at the junction and the car park is 600 metres up on the left

https://www.wikiloc.com/hiking-trails/pinsapos-plus-34611091

WALK 130 GRAZALEMA - TORREON AND THE GARGANTA VERDE – 2 SHORT WALKS IN ONE DAY

Time: 2.5 hours each (6 Kilometres)
Difficulty: moderate
Terrain: rocky paths

BRIEF DESCRIPTION. Torreon is the highest peak in Cadiz province and the vews are well worth the stiff climb and the scrambling near the top
HOW TO GET THERE On A372 Grazalema/ El Bosque road
NB permit needed from park authorities for both walks.
email: cv_elbosque@agenciamedioambienteyagua.es (15 days' notice required!)
telephone: 956 70 97 33 (Centro de visitantes P.N Sierra de Grazalema (El Bosque). You can also collect a permit for the Torreon in Grazalema Tourist Office.
https://www.wikiloc.com/hiking-trails/subida-al-torreon-grazalema-cadiz-25-may-14-30110718

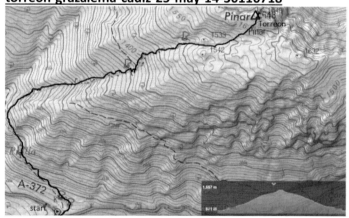

THE WALK: from the car park simply take the path which goes straight to the top. Return the same way.

GARGANTA VERDE

BRIEF DESCRIPTION: A spectacular walk whIch descends into the Garganta Verde where the Ballesteros stream has eroded the mountainside into a deep cleft. The path returns the same way .

https://www.wikiloc.com/hiking-trails/hike-into-the-garganta-verde-7-km-25245239

Access is from Zahara /Grazalema on CA 9104 at K10

THE WALK: From the car park join the path which initially skirts the side of the gorge. At MAP 1 there is a side path leading to a viewpoint. At MAP 2 The path starts the descent. At MAP 3 there are steps with railings; reach the riverbed at MAP 4. Pass a hermitage at MAP 5 and the path terminates at MAP 6. Retrace your steps.

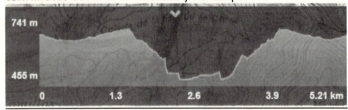

WALK 131   BENAOCAZ – TO JAULETAS

Time: 6 hours excluding summit (7 including summit) (11K)
Difficulty: hard due to terrain
Terrain: rough paths overgrown in places

BRIEF DESCRIPTION: a stunning walk in the wilds of the Grazalema Natural Park on little used paths, but with a gentle return over open grassy plains. It is strongly recommended to use the wikiloc track.

HOW TO GET THERE: Benaocaz is on the A374 between Ubrique and Villaluenga . Park next to Posada El Parral at west end of village.

THE WALK: go to the left of the hotel down a concrete ramp then down steps to a track leading off the road to the right. It has a sign Saltero du Cabrera. Pass some farm buildings and the track reduces to a path, crosses an ancient bridge and at MAP 1, 200 metres from the bridge, turn right off the main path up a rough path opposite a metal gate on the left. This is 1 kilometre from the start. Pass through two gates then at 2,2 kilometres from the start keep straight on where there is a hint of a path to the right (MAP 2). 600 metres later take a small rocky path to the left marked by a cairn (MAP 3) which zigzags up the side of the mountain, over a ridge and then follows a series of wooded glades along a valley heading north. At K3.2 from the start, take care to keep right of rocks that appear to block the way. (MAP 4) I have placed a cairn to help. Keep going up the gully now increasingly rocky and difficult to follow but you will pass close to a rocky outcrop.

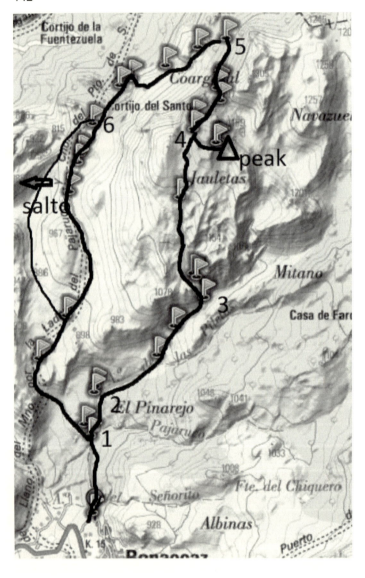

https://www.wikiloc.com/hiking-trails/walk-book-5-walk-131-benaocaz-las-jauletas-47739883

Continue north until K4.3 from the start, where you reach a small glade with a tree with a split in the trunk (MAP 5). From here you can head east up rocky slabs to the summit of Jauletas; allow 30 minutes each way. From MAP 5 continue north passing a solitary stick on the ridge. From here you start descending in a north east direction, then when you reach an open area, veer left to climb a ridge and then pass over the top (MAP 6).

There are cairns to help find your way. 100 metres the other side, pass by a metal grill and some barbed wire and descend for 400 metres, when veer sharp left to head south west (MAP 7).

Keep left after a further 200 metres where there is a hint of a split in the path. Reassuring landmarks on the next section are firstly, a stone built abandoned corral then a circular rock cut water trough, which heralds an easier section of path (MAP 8). When you arrive at a wall, edge left through a gate by a stone barn and then drop down to join a more substantial path coming from the right. Turn left and uphill when it soon forks left and passes by a cluster of signs. (MAP 9)

The terrain becomes much more open and the path is easier to follow, now heading south; (an ancient drovers right of way) you just need to be careful to leave a farm to your left (MAP 10), then a second farm also well to your left (MAP 11), to ensure you pass through the right hand of two openings in the hillside ahead. The path then descends steeply towards Benaocaz ahead of you. (MAP 12) It passes by another farm with friendly donkeys and pigs before you rejoin the path you started the walk on. You are 15 minutes from the finish.

WALK 132   VILLALUENGA – RELOJ/SIMANCON

Time: 6-7 hours (14 kilometres)
Difficulty: hard
Terrain: mainly rocky paths and open mountainside
BRIEF DESCRIPTION: A truly spectacular walk taking in two of the main peaks of the Grazalema Natural Park, following little used but easy to follow shepherd´s paths. There is a tricky descent on a rocky path to finish.
HOW TO GET THERE: Villaluenga is on the A374 between Ubrique and Grazalema. Park in the main car park at the north end of the village.
THE WALK: from the roundabout by the car park take the steep street up the right side of the housing and turn right along a paved walkway along the side of the steep cliffs. 1500 metres from the start, turn left through a wire and post gate (MAP 1) and then follow a rocky path marked by cairns going diagonally up the slope to reach a gate in a wall (MAP 2). Head towards a gap in the mountainside and then enter a valley running at right angles to your heading. Once in the valley, when you reach some farm buildings (MAP 3), keep left to climb up the valley floor to reach a gate in a wall. Turn immediately right (MAP 4) and head up to a pine wood passing through a gap in the wall after a few minutes. Zigzag up the hill for about 20 minutes and when you reach a junction of paths, turn right (MAP 5). This path leads you over attractive flattish landscape towards the towering mass of El Reloj. After 1500 metres it reaches the foot of Reloj by a pond to your left. Keep straight on to follow cairns up the mountain, turning off the path when it veers right down a slope (MAP 6). Frequent cairns guide you to the summit as there is no clear footpath. https://www.wikiloc.com/hiking-trails/walk-book-5-walk-132-reloj-simancon-47739452

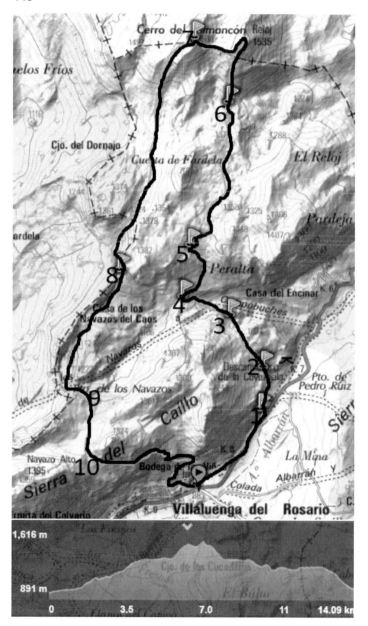

Visit the right hand of the two peaks first (Reloj), although you could miss this out by diverting to the left peak of Simancon just before the summit across a spur connecting the two peaks. The ascent of Simancon is a matter of following cairns placed by previous visitors which are of considerable help. The views from Simancon are immense (MAP 7), with a 360 degree vista, being higher than Reloj at 1565 metres. From the summit head northwest towards the second of two gaps to your left (the wikiloc track goes down through the first gap on a rougher route). The path through the second gap is clearer and marked with cairns. At the bottom of this slope the path flattens out, passes through rocks then enters a high grassy plain. At the end it passes through a gap and descends through bushes and trees to a wall and gate at the bottom.

Near the bottom you pass by a water trough. After a gate, veer left along a narrow path which rises up to reach a gate in the wall (MAP 8). On the other side the path splits after a few metres. Turn right down a steep slope which leads to a grassy area where a path runs alongside the steep side on your right heading south. You climb out of this hollow and continue into a long valley again surrounded on both sides by steep sided rock faces. The mass of a large mountain (El Navazo) faces you. As you start rising again the path edges left, to climb through a gap and reach a plateau with a grassy plain ahead. (MAP 9) Now aim for the lowest point at the far end of this plain where you join a rocky footpath which climbs a few metres to pass through the gap (MAP 10) and then head east around the side of a mountain to your left. This path leads you down to Villaluenga which will appear below you. Turn left at the bottom when you reach the village to return to the car park.

WALK 133 JIMENA - VULTURES ROCK POOLS AND ROCK SLABS

Time: 4 hours (11 Kilometres)
Difficulty: moderate (wikiloc track recommended)
Terrain: rough tracks, rough paths, rock scrambling

BRIEF DESCRIPTION: A great summer walk, with swimming in the rock pool. Spectacular scenery in a particularly wild part of the Alcornocales. Some rock scrambling after you leave the gorge on the return section.

HOW TO GET THERE: Drive south of Jimena on the A405 for 5 kilometres. At a white and blue venta at Marchenillas on the left, turn right down a track, cross the river on a ford and park just the other side of the railway crossing.

THE WALK: from your car, turn right and go 50 metres to a gate (MAP 1). On the other side, turn left up a rough track leading up the hill. After 700 metres turn left (MAP 2) and follow this track over the brow and down the other side towards a lake heading due south. The track first loops past a ruin then crosses over another track after 500 metres then after another 250 metres go right off the track on a cow path keeping your heading south towards the lake. Some 50 metres before the lake, (MAP 3) turn right on to a track and follow it into trees and bushes. It reduces to a path and then drops down to a stream (the Salado) by a black pipe. Cross over and veer right up a path which climbs up to a rocky area overlooking a pool and a waterfall (MAP 4).
https://www.wikiloc.com/hiking-trails/walk-book-jimena-book-6-walk-18-salado-valley-definitive-route-43340877

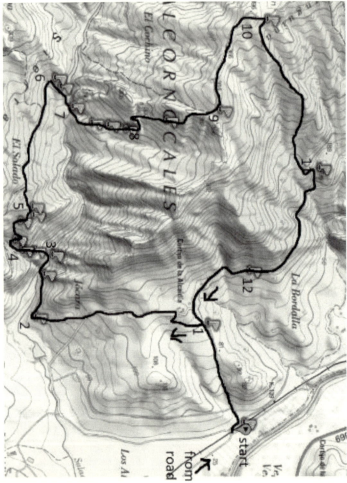

The path continues to climb the rock face (a bit of scrambling required) and then turns sharp left to climb a more open area with scattered cork trees marked by the occasional cairn. The path crosses over the top, drops down the other side for 50 metres, then it edges right, up a cleft in the rock face to join a gully on its right-hand side (MAP 5). When you reach a large metal cage / small, fenced enclosure, overgrown inside, veer right to follow a cairn-marked path which zigzags up the hill, a little indistinctly in places.

200 metres from the cage at a more open area, veer right just beyond a forked cork tree to head north through bushes for 200 metres, where there is a neolithic tomb to the right. (It is hard to spot). A few metres further on turn left up a bank to enter an open grassy area with a ruin on the left almost obscured by brambles (MAP 6). Head to the top right-hand corner and pass through a wall in trees on a small path which will lead you along the left side of the Salado valley through thick woods to a long stretch of rocks leading to the stream at the bottom of the gorge. Occasional cairns will guide you.

When you emerge from the woods you meet a path just before a flat rock face (MAP 7). Go right and after 50 metres go through bushes to the left on to the slab and cairns will lead you across and then down the rocky slope to the stream below. Enjoy a swim in the deep rock pool to the left, (MAP 8) then follow the stream on the left for 50 metres and cut left where the rock face finishes. Go up a gully for a few metres and climb up the side of a rock face on the right. Go left up through bushes then onto the rock slab for 200 metres heading north always keeping on the left side of the rockface. Then cross the gully through bushes ahead and climb up the side of the larger rock face again heading north. After 50 metres at a small dip in the rock face drop down to the left and then go right to follow a spur to head north again.

When you join a wider spur there is a bush filled gully to your left (MAP 9). You now need to turn left down this spur for 50 metres until the bushes start to thin out and then turn right to join a massive rockface which you climb.

There is a strange collection of large boulders to your left and then you pass by a large cave also to your left. At the top of this section there is a bush-filled gully in front of you marked by a cairn. Drop into the gully and go straight across onto another rock face opposite. Go up to locate a point where you can drop down into a larger open area with a fence on the left side.

Keep going straight up this scrubby area and there is a rockface on your right converging with the fence on your left. Go right when you reach a cleft in the rockface and a cairn above will confirm your position. Skirt round the right side of this rocky mound all the time gaining height. Then leave this rocky area to veer left towards the fence and a bushy path will lead you between the fence and the rock face towards a track which is beyond a gate at top of the fence 50 metres further on (MAP 10).
Turn left and follow the track along the ridge heading north west for just over a kilometre. At a junction (MAP 11) turn right down the hill and head north east for 1200 metres to meet a track at the bottom. Just before the bottom after the track has turned left and is rising towards the gates of a house, (MAP 12) turn right by a black pipe and drop down a wide rough path to the track below. Turn right and follow the contour line for another 1200 metres where you climb a padlocked gate (MAP 13). The track is rougher the other side where you pass a barn on your right then re-join the track you began the walk on. Continue down the hill, turning right through the gate at the bottom to reach your car.

WALK 134 CASTILLO DE CASTELLAR TO THE CUEVA DE LOS MAQUIS

Time: 4.5 hours (13 Kilometres) including visit to cave
Difficulty: easy
Terrain: paths and tracks

BRIEF DESCRIPTION: A fascinating walk starting from the historic castle complex of Castillo de Castellar and taking in rock drawings and the Cueva (Cave) de los Maquis. See this website for photos and information about the drawings https://www.prehistoriadelsur.com/2013/12/cueva-de-los-maquis-1.html
You will also enjoy great views across the reservoir of Guadarranque and the local countryside.

HOW TO GET THERE: From the A405 Jimena to San Roque road, take the exit signposted to Castillo de Castellar from the roundabout at Almoraima, there is a cork yard nearby. Drive up to the first car park below the castle on the left.
THE WALK: with the castle behind you take a grassy path in the left corner going downhill past a couple of bungalows. When you reach the road below turn left and walk up the road to the next left-hand bend and take a paved path to the right downhill (MAP 1). You shortly reach a mirador; turn right to follow the GR7 and SL 115 downhill for 15 minutes or so. (Calzada de la Boyal) The path meets the road at the bottom of the hill (MAP 2). Cross straight over and at a white arrow painted on the barrier, climb over to join a path the other side which drops down to emerge back on the road by the Venta La Jarandilla, then turn right just past the venta on to a tarmac road and cross a bridge (MAP 3). 300 metres later, keep left at a fork and shortly pass through a metal gate. (or round the left-hand wall

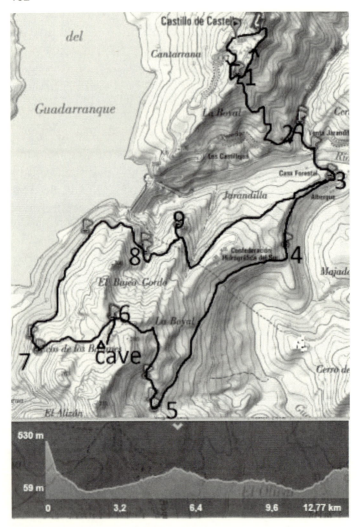

https://es.wikiloc.com/rutas-a-pie/castellar-to-the-cueva-de-los-maquis-31161152

if padlocked) 500 metres after the gate take a right fork (MAP 4).

1500 metres later (MAP 5), turn right up an obvious wide path between bushes heading due north back towards Castillo de Castellar, passing a pond on your left. Then veer left to a white pump house where the path now climbs into rocks and trees. Then head west to the Riscos de los Bazanos. As you approach a long slab of rock on your left, take a small path to the left to take you up to the rock paintings and the Cueva del Maquis. (MAP 6) You will have to go on a very narrow path between the bushes and the long slab to go up to the top. (Not on the wikilocs track) Return to the main path turning left descending gradually making sure you keep right where there is a fork (MAP 7) (cairn here) and then drop down to a track where you turn right. Follow the road as it skirts the side of the reservoir. As you approach the dam keep on the main track which becomes tarmacked. When you reach a padlocked gate, drop down to the left and pass over a trampled down fence and turn right on to the lower road which passes through open gates. (MAP 8) If shut, you can climb over the wall to the right. Continue round the side of the hill where there is a mirador on your left (MAP 9). Pass a turn off on the right to an office building and later rejoin the track on which you began this part of the walk.

When you reach the Venta turn left and take the footpath off to the left. Take the left fork after crossing the stream and this will lead you up to the road. Cross straight over and take the cobbled path you started the walk on. At the mirador go straight on up to visit the fascinating castle complex, (formerly the village of Castellar which was relocated when the reservoir was built in the 1960s) or turn left to rejoin your car in the lower car park.

WALK 135 SENDERO MARAPOSA MONARCA RETURN VIA ARROYO ARRANDILLA AND ALMORAIMA

Time: 5 hours (18 kilometres)
Difficulty: moderate
Terrain: paths, tracks

BRIEF DESCRIPTION: a varied, relatively gentle walk, initially along the banks of the river Guadarranque, where you have a good chance of sighting the Monarch butterfly.

Later you ascend the valley of the Arrandilla stream, then enter the state owned Almoraima estate, pass through cork woods then finish via the new village of Castellar de la Frontera.

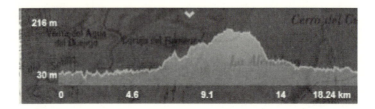

HOW TO GET THERE: the walk starts at the Venta La Cantina which is on the A405 Gaucin to San Roque road just south of the Almoraima/Castellar roundabout

THE WALK: take the wide track to the right of the Venta La Cantina and just before the bridge take the path between two posts to the right (MAP 1). You drop down to the river which you then follow for 5.2 kilometres, either on a track

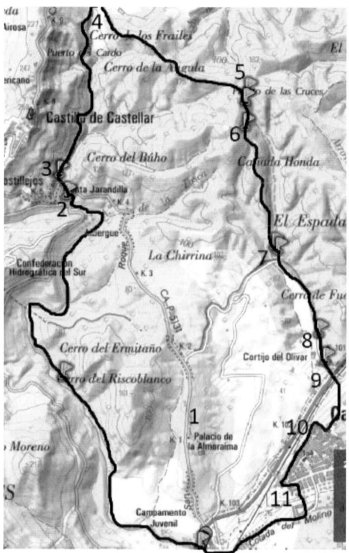

https://www.wikiloc.com/hiking-trails/book-5-walkl-135-castellar-ruta-amaposa-monarca-return-via-arrandilla-and-almoraima-special-walks-i-32048000 or on a narrower path. There are occasional marker posts but often there is more than one option; if in doubt keep as close as you can to the riverbank. Do keep your eyes open for the glorious Monarch butterfly, my wikiloc track has a photo of one taken when I did the walk in January.

After 5 kilometres you emerge at the side of a track leading out to a tarmac road with the Venta Jarrandilla 100 metres to your left (MAP 2). Walk past the venta and up the road. After a bend to the left and a bridge over a stream, take a small path to the right just beyond the bridge, marked by a faded sign saying Camino de difficultad media (MAP 3). This will take you a further 3 kilometres or so up this wooded valley, meandering in and out of side gullies but generally keeping on the left-hand side of the stream. The path occasionally splits but always rejoins, so dont worry about losing your way.

Eventually the path emerges from the woods onto a flatter grassy area and meets a track coming from a gate on your right (MAP 4). Turn right and either climb the gate if padlocked or squeeze under the fence to the right. You are entering the publicly owned Almoraima estate, so you have a right of way. Follow the track as it enters woods climbing a little, ignoring any side turnings, and 2.3 kilometres from the gate, reach a junction of tracks with a broken waymark post in the apex of the junction (MAP 5). Fork right here and then after 100 metres keep left. Then after a further 300 metres take the left fork down a slightly less used track which leads downhill (MAP 6). At the bottom the track arrives at an open flat area with various tracks leading off. Keep in the same direction back into trees and you will find a padlocked gate, the other side of which is a concrete water channel with a bridge (MAP 7). There is a way through the fence to the left of the gate. Cross the bridge and turn left onto a concrete track alongside the channel.

Exactly one kilometre from the bridge (MAP 8), you fork right off the concrete track leaving a building (a cemetery) to your right and pass by a wall across the track to enter the access road to the cemetery. Turn left and shortly arrive at the main road which may be busy (MAP 9). Cross over and then cross the railway to reach a track which passes between avocado plantations going right at the fork just beyond the railway line. The track leads south to the village of Castellar de la Frontera.

When you arrive at housing the best way round the village is to veer right and follow the Calle La Linea which skirts the right-hand side (MAP 10). When you reach a road, which is entering the village from the right across a bridge over the main road, go straight over and down the slope towards a football stadium (MAP 11). Turn left on to a dual carriage way, go 200 metres and turn right onto Calle Las Rosas. At the end, turn right onto a road which takes you out of the village to the village of Almoraima. Turn right at the next junction, cross the railway and then turn right onto the main road to reach the Venta La Cantina 100 metres up on the left where there are refreshments.

WALK 136 - CASTILLO DE CASTELLAR

Time: 4.5 hours (11 kilometres)

Diffculty: easy

Terrain: mainly paths, a section of gravel track

BRIEF DESCRIPTION: a gem of a walk containing all the ingredients you want from a good walk: views, good paths, architectural and archaeological interest, varied scenery and ease of navigation.

HOW TO GET THERE: from the Almoraima roundabout on the A405 Gaucin to San Roque road, take the turn off to Castillo de Castellar. At K4.5 (Venta Jarandilla) park in the large car park on the left.

THE WALK: walk up the same road and after the next bend, and a bridge, turn right off the road onto a small path by a wooden sign. (MAP 1) Go left immediately at a fork in the path and climb the slope. Now follow the path up the left-hand side of the valley for just under 3 kilometres, until you reach an open area with a fence to your right. (MAP 2)

At a sign in a tree saying Castillo pointing to the left, go left into the bushes on a narrow path. 100 metres later there is a panel board describing a neolithic tomb up a path to the left. This is worth a detour (MAP 3). Return to the path and continue up the hill to a gravel track. Turn right, go 100 metres and take the first path to the left into bushes (MAP 4). Soon pass by a ruined house with a panel board, keep left, then at a fork in the path, keep right.

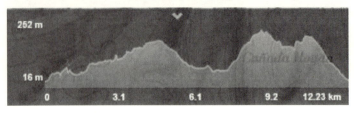

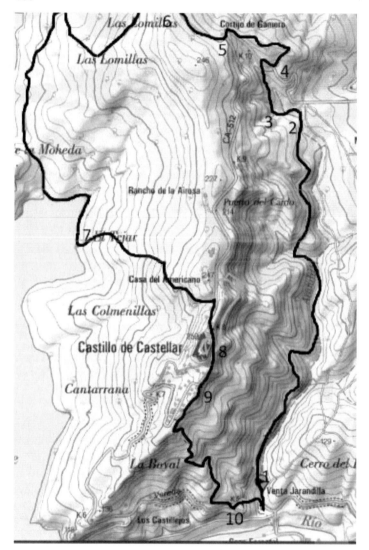

https://www.wikiloc.com/hiking-trails/walk-136-from-book-special-walks-in-southern-andalucia-castillo-de-castellar-35885500

Then pass to the left of a barn up the slope and turn right along a track. (MAP 5)

After 300 metres turn left off the track down a less well-maintained track which loops down the hill towards a large reservoir below (MAP 6). It veers left and then reduces to a grassy path on a grassy slope. The now rather faint path passes through trees down to the water´s edge. Follow the edge of the lake until you reach a wall with a tree to the left of the wall (MAP 7).

Proceed up the slope past a tree with a sign pinned to the trunk and pick up a rough path which climbs up into trees. 400 metres later pass by an interesting water source in a vaulted building. Leave it to your left and join a paved stone path heading towards the mass of the castle complex of Castellar. Turn right on to the road and then take a stroll round the historic fortifications (MAP 8).

Then return to the road and drop down to the left of the castle until you reach a paved stone path on your left. (MAP 9) This path goes straight down the hill marked as the GR7 past a mirador and rejoins the road at the bottom. (MAP 10)

Cross straight over, mount the metal barrier with a white arrow and go down the narrow path to cross the streambed and rejoin the road just by the Venta Jarandilla where your car is parked.

WALK 137 CASTELLAR - CAÑADA DE JARAL AND TORRETA DEL MORO

Time: 5 hours (15.5 kilometres)
Difficulty: moderate
Terrain: mainly tracks, section of rough paths through woods

BRIEF DESCRIPTION: A magnificent walk entirely in the publicly owned Almoraima estate. Views to all points of the compass, including Castillo de Castellar. In theory permission is needed to enter but this would mean hiring a guide, so I suggest not to bother. This walk is walk 22 from Guia de Excursionistas del Campo de Gibraltar which makes no mention of permission needed.

HOW TO GET THERE: on the A405 San Roque to Gaucin road, take the track to the right of the Venta La Cantina 50 metres south of the roundabout with the turn off to Castillo de Castellar; go to the end of the track where there is a padlocked gate. Park here.

THE WALK: Climb the fence to the left of the gates, a pallet will facilitate this and follow the track for 400 metres. Turn left at the junction, cross a streambed and go immediately right (MAP 1) up the left side of the stream over open ground and after 200 metres, go half left up the second opening on the slope on a path that becomes paved with stones (MAP 2), which is the path to follow for 2 kilometres through woods. From time to time the paved path is hard to follow due to neglect and encroaching undergrowth but keep following the general direction of west, then southwest. 1500 metres from the start of the path you cross a stream bed, veer right to head northwest then

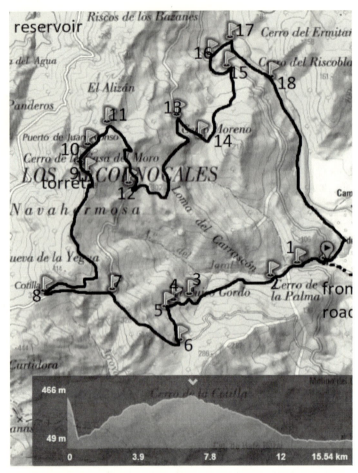

https://www.wikiloc.com/hiking-trails/walk-book-5-walk-137-torreta-el-moro-42205532

arrive at a shoulder with a choice of routes (MAP 3). Turn 90 degrees left here and head up the slope on a small path which soon shows signs of the paved path again. Pass two fallen cork oaks before emerging on to open ground where you edge slightly left up the firebreak (MAP 4) to reach a rough track 200 metres further up. (MAP 5)

Turn left and go to the end of the track which joins a well-made track where you turn right (MAP 6). You now follow this track for 1 kilometre keeping left at a junction, (MAP 7) then after 800 metres turn right up a rougher track (MAP 8) which doubles back parallel to the previous track before climbing for 2 kilometres to reach the skeletal remains of the Torreta del Moro (MAP 9).

200 metres past the Torreta, edge right at open area where there is residue of tree felling (MAP 10). You drop down through trees on to a ridge which you follow for 500 metres before bearing right now heading south west (MAP 11). After 1 kilometre turn left (MAP 12), then 1500 metres later turn right (MAP 13). This track approaches an open area to the left after 300 metres (MAP 14), whereupon you turn left down a faint track which heads back north down a very rough track to reach a tarmacked road in poor condition (MAP 15).

Turn left and go just 300 metres and as the road veers left uphill (MAP 16), go down the slope to the right to join a rough path following the right bank of a stream. You emerge on to a track where you turn right with the river Guadarranque below to your left (MAP 17). This track will lead you back to the start as you long as you take the right hand track of three, when it splits after 500 metres (MAP 18). At a later point again take the right-hand track at a fork some 300 metres before the end of the walk. When you cross a streambed turn left to rejoin your car.

WALK 138 – CASTELLAR TO THE PINAR DEL REY

Time: 4 hours (16 Kilometres)
Difficulty: easy
Terrain: mainly sandy paths and tracks; one descent on rocky path

BRIEF DESCRIPTION: a surprisingly attractive walk in the Pinar del Rey, a local beauty spot very popular with the locals. Avoid weekends if you like peace and quiet.

HOW TO GET THERE: take the A405 San Roque to Gaucin and 200 metres south of the roundabout with the turn off to Castillo de Castellar turn towards Castellar, cross the railway and park in the trees on the right 50 metres on by a sports pitch.

THE WALK: leaving the sports ground to your left follow a gravel track up the hill passing through a gate after 500 metres. Take the left fork where the track splits. After 400 metres at MAP 1 take a narrower track to the right and downhill for 200 metres, heading south, where you veer left when the path splits. Cross a stream on a wooden bridge and veer right when you meet a path (MAP 2) then keep right at the next junction and veer left when you meet a path coming from the right. 2.7 kilometres into the walk you arrive at a wide gravel track (MAP 3). Turn left and go 500 metres due east and when you reach a gate, pass through and turn right along a sandy track for about 200 metres where you turn left through a gap in the fence the other side of which is a large irrigation canal.
Cross the bridge and turn right to follow the canal to the next bridge, where you leave the canal, pass through a wire and post gate to the left, and turn right on a sandy track.

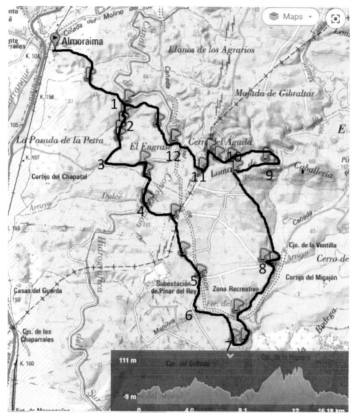

(MAP 4) This soon veers left and climbs the slope to reach a fence below large pylons. Turn right, go a few metres and veer left through a gate to reach a wide firebreak. Cross over and a few metres downhill take a path heading into the woods on the left marked by a way post. Go south for 500 metres then edge left, then right now heading south east for a further 400 metres to a gate leading to a wide gravel track (MAP 5). Go through the pedestrian gate to the right and join the wide track to head south. As you pass under more pylons turn left on to a sandy firebreak and head east following the pylons (MAP 6) (the wikiloc track cuts the corner).

After 500 metres turn right and continue to the bottom of the slope to an open area (MAP 7). Turn left and go about 100 metres to meet a path ahead. Turn left heading north and follow this path until you reach a display board where you keep right. Go a further 700 metres until you reach a gap in the fence ahead. Pass through, drop down a bank and turn left and 100 metres to meet a fence and a display board the other side (MAP 8). Turn right here to follow a wide sandy firebreak down the hill. Ignore one turn to the left and then take the next turn to the left up a sandy firebreak (Kilometre 9 of the walk).

Go 1.4 kilometres climbing gradually, then take a path to the right marked by a way post. This leads to a rocky summit from which there are great views and a good picnic spot (MAP 9). Leaving the rocks to your right continue downhill on a rocky path which turns left to follow the valley floor. You rejoin the sandy firebreak where you turn right and after just a few metres turn left on to a forest path (MAP 10). Head west climbing gently until you reach a fence and a line of pylons. Turn left and follow the fence downhill into a wide gully and locate a flap in the fence which you can lift up and climb through (MAP 11). Head down this gully on a rough path for 400 metres veering right further down to head north for a few minutes and when you can see a quarry to the right and the canal below edge left and drop down to the canal and cross the bridge. (MAP 12) Opposite there is a gate on a track which you pass through, go 100 metres and turn right on to a good track. Go just under 1.5 kilometres heading north, then west to rejoin your outward route at MAP 1. Keep straight on to return to your car.

https://www.wikiloc.com/hiking-trails/pinar-del-rey-from-castellar-57823317

WALK 139 - GIBRALTAR - MEDITERRANEAN STEPS AND THE CHARLES V WALL

Time: 4 hours allowing for frequent stops (7 Kilometres)
Difficulty: moderate
Terrain: roads paths and stone steps

BRIEF DESCRIPTION: a most unusual walk, based on the historic Mediterranean Steps up the east cliff face of the Rock of Gibraltar, and a descent of the Charles V wall, recently restored and reopened. Also included is the new Royal Anglian Way suspension bridge and a walk through a nature reserve. Note the Gibraltar tourist websites state that a ticket is required to visit the upper rock on foot. However, in all my years of walking around Gibraltar I have never been asked for a ticket. This route goes nowhere near any check-points so my advice is to plead ignorance if challenged.
Extract from http://www.visitgibraltar.gi/nature-reserve-info
There are two categories of prices, whether you simply wish to walk the reserve and enjoy the nature trails, wildlife and views or include the history and majestic caves and tunnels in your visit

Ticket Prices: Walk the Gibraltar Nature Reserve, Upper Rock
(excluding attractions): £5

HOW TO GET THERE: from the frontier cross the airport runway and take the following roads: Winston Churchill, then right on to Glacis Road, then Queensway Road to Ragged Staff Gates. Left through the wall, then follow signs to Europa Point. Pass the Rock Hotel, and 1 kilometre further on turn left up Windmill Hill Road, signposted to the Upper Rock. Just past a sharp left-hand bend on the right hand side there is an industrial building with wasteland alongside with plenty of parking. Leave your car here.

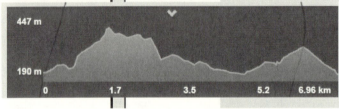

https://www.wikiloc.com/hiking-trails/walk-138-from-book-special-walks-in-southern-andalucia-gibraltar-med-steps-35131207

THE WALK: continue up Windmill Hill Road and after a sharp left-hand bend locate the entrance to the Jewish Cemetery. It is about 50 metres before a barrier across the road and just before open metal gates. Go up the metal walkway and past a water tap in the style of a fountain, then left up some metal steps and at the top of the steps go through a metal gate and walk past the graves up the slope into some trees where there is a small path. 10 metres later you emerge on to a well-maintained path. Turn right (MAP 1). You are now on the Mediterranean Steps. (this route circumvents the need to pay 5 pounds to enter the upper rock on foot.) If you wish to pay the 5 pounds, then go past the barrier and pay at the kiosk and then turn right up a path.

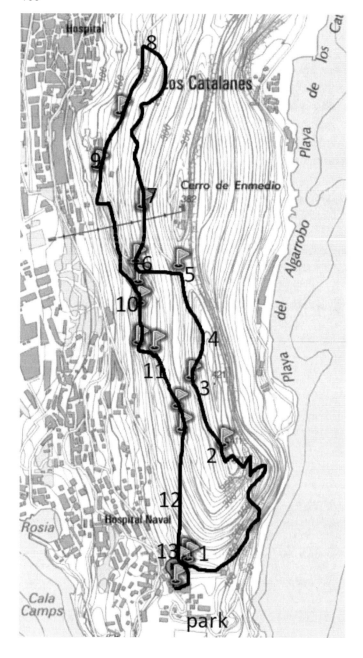

Now follow this path as it skirts round to the east side of the rock, passes through a tunnel, then starts a virtiginous zigzag climb. After 45 minutes or so you emerge at the top near O´Haras Battery, 100 metres to your left (MAP 2). Turn sharp right down O´Haras road, (left for an interesting visit to the impressive gun emplacement) and almost immediately keep left, then after 400 metres leave the road and bear right up Douglas Path (MAP 3).

This takes you to Douglas Lookout and then returns you to the road, now called St Michaels Road. The Gibraltar Skywalk is here (MAP 4). Turn right and continue until you reach the top of Charles V Wall (MAP 5) passing a viewing point on the way.

Go down the steps of the wall and after three sections arrive at Queens road. Keep the road on your left and immediately bear right on to a gravel path called Inglis Way. (MAP 6)

After 300 metres, before you reach a road (Charles Vth Road), turn left on to a path (MAP 7), which descends into woods and gradually loses height. You then rise a little along a fence before dropping steeply to emerge on to Queens Road by Brice´s farm where you turn left (MAP 8). You soon reach a junction. Fork right ono Old Queens Road and then when you reach Green Lane emerging from the right, cross over the road to enter the Gibraltar Nature Reserve a few metres to the left of the junction. (MAP 9)

The path follows the contour line then veers left to climb some steps to emerge onto the road. Turn right. Continue past Apes Den and the Charles V Wall. After 100 metres, turn right off the road on to the Royal Anglian Way, part of the Upper Rock Nature reserve. E on map below. (MAP 10) First cross the new Windsor suspension bridge, then pass Haynes Cave Battery.

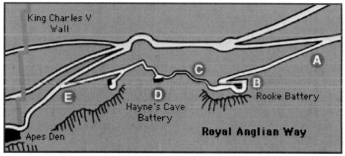

MAP SHOWING ROYAL ANGLIAN WAY

Just before Rooke Battery (B on map of Royal Anglian Way), take the steps leading up the rock to emerge near a junction. Turn left and at the junction take the sharp right fork leading to St Michaels Cave (There is a sign) (MAP 11). When you reach the cave, keep right and just past the cave buildings, on the lower road, take a path leading right downhill . (MAP 12)

After about 400 metres cross over a road and after a further 200 metres, just before a road, turn left to find the start of the Mediterranean steps. There is a panel board here displaying a brief history and a map. (MAP 13) If you have a ticket then drop down to the road and turn left to rejoin your car. Otherwise go past the Med steps panel board and take the path a few metres on the right down to the Jewish Cemetery.

WALK 140 LOS BARRIOS – BACINETE - TOMBS AND ROCK PAINTINGS

Time: 5 hours 30 minutes (15 kilometres)
Difficulty: easy
Terrain: Track and rough paths and final section on a quiet road. One river crossing, the bridge has been washed away in 2018. Avoid this walk after heavy rain.

BRIEF DESCRIPTION: this is an interesting walk as it includes a visit to primitive rock drawings and neolithic tombs as well as enjoying views of the hills of the southern part of the Alcornocales Natural Park. In theory, permission is needed from the landowner of the Finca La Dehesa but no further details are given on the website http://www.dipucadiz.es/desarrollo_sostenible/senderos/Santuario-de-Bacinete/Anotherwebsite http://www.rutasyfotos.com/2010/01/santuario-de-bacinete.html (which has great photos of the drawings and tombs) offers these numbers as a point of contact 956236480 or 956622700 but then admits the phone has never answered!! A further possibility is to contact the tourist office of Los Barrios through this website http://turismolosbarrios.com/diviertete/senderismo/
I have visited at least 5 times without incident over the years without even realising that permission is needed. (most recently in 2018 when the bridge carrying the GR7 path has been washed away.)
HOW TO GET THERE: Take the A381 and leave at exit 80. Go north on the C440a and park at the Venta El Frenazo just under a kilometre up the road on the right -hand side.
https://www.wikiloc.com/walking-trails/walk-book-5-walk-139-bacinete-and-gr-7-special-walks-in-s-andalucia-30884653

THE WALK: Cross over and take the country road opposite the venta which goes under the motorway and then crosses the river Palmones. This is the GR7. After passing two farms 1500 metres from the start take the right fork, (MAP 1) and go about 1.2 kilometres further where you then leave the track on a path off to the right following a fence (MAP 2). This path is just beyond a padlocked gate on the right. Walk parallel to the track on your left, pass by a small mirador with a panel board (MAP 3) and after 150 metres, rejoin the track again. After 600 metres take the right fork off the main track after passing one track to the right leading to a small farm (MAP 4). You then go between some farm buildings and pass an abandoned tractor. before reaching a stream, having passed through a couple of wire and post gates. At the stream there are red and white banded posts indicating the GR7 footpath. (MAP 5) Cross the stream as best you can, as in 2018 the footbridge has been washed away leaving a length of steel wire. We went upstream about 50 metres and found a shallower wider route with an island and helpful trees. Climb the bank and turn left to rejoin the path and then follow the stream for about 500 metres. Leave the stream through a wire and post gate and then head west, leaving the GR 7 which is indicated by cairns (MAP 6). Climb up, on a grassy track used by vehicles, to a gate the other side of which is a well-maintained track (MAP 7). Turn right (looking out for cyclists) and after 300 metres turn left through a metal gate or climb over the stile (MAP 8).
Follow the track, edging right, for 200 metres then turn left through a gate and head up the hill edging right off the track until you reach a ladder stile which you climb over. (MAP 9) The now rocky path goes through bushes and trees to arrive first at massive rock structures behind which

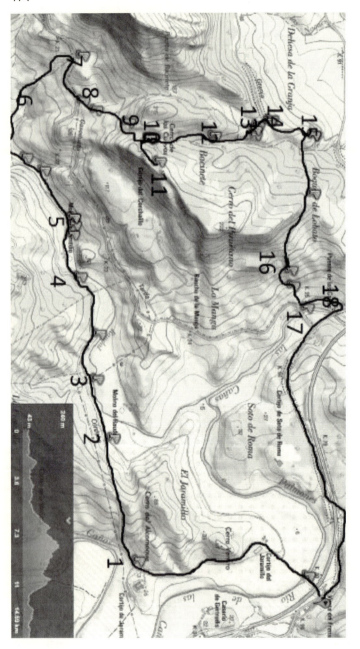

the rock drawings carved in a hollowed out rock, protected by railings (MAP 10). To reach the tombs, take a rough path up the slope and pass two massive slabs. The ten or so tombs are carved out of the rock on the ground (MAP 11). Then retrace your steps and leave the large rocks to your left to locate a foot path heading north and down the slope to take you to a track 700 metres down the hill. This path is not easy to follow but if you follow the cairns and stay on the left-hand side of the gully you wont be too far wrong. At one point (500 metres from the rocks), turn right down the slope and then left to remain in the gully (MAP 12). Watch out for cairns. The path eventually reaches an abandoned building which you leave to your left (MAP 13), then veer left to pass through gorse bushes to reach a very rough track where you turn right. 100 metres later, pass through a gate (MAP 14), ignoring a track going off to the right, go 50 metres and turn right through another gate.

Go 400 metres, through a wire and post gate, and then turn right off the track (MAP 15) along a firebreak which reaches a streambed which you cross. On the other side join a rough track and climb the slope to reach a radio mast and an abandoned building. Here, join a concrete track leading down the other side of the hill. 600 metres from the building, after a couple of bends turn left down a line of pylons on a rough path (MAP 16). 100 metres down, veer left and then downhill through a field to a fence in the bottom right-hand corner. Climb the fence and then turn left onto a track (actually a public cycle track) (MAP 17) and head to a gate leading to a car park. At the end turn right down a little used tarmacked road, the former Los Barrios to Jerez road now replaced by an autovia (MAP 15). It is 2 kilometres to your car.

WALK 141   ALGECIRAS - CABECERA RIO DE LA MIEL

Time: 5 hours (16 Kilometres)
Difficulty: moderate
Terrain: tracks and paths

BRIEF DESCRIPTION: A walk in the Alcornocales Natural Park just outside Algeciras with views of Gibraltar and of the hinterland behind Algeciras: the return is down the valley of the Rio del Miel. There is a bathing spot near the end of the walk.

HOW TO GET THERE: From Algeciras head for the Barrio El Cobre from exit 105 on the N340/A7 ring road. Turn right off the slip road then left at the next roundabout. Climb up through housing and after passing over the top take the second exit at the roundabout and head down the hill on Calle Escritora Juana Marin. At the next roundabout take the second exit and then merge with a road from your left, pass a bar on your left and a street with a no entry sign. Then take the next left and follow as it becomes Calle Muera Curro. Park where there is a turning area. The gate for the start of the walk is here.

THE WALK: Go through the metal gate along a path to join a track (turn right) passing through open countryside. After just under 800 metres take the left fork up a minor track when the track splits. (MAP 1) (You will return along the right fork which leads to the rio Del Miel.)
This track climbs gradually. After 400 metres (MAP 2), turn right onto a path which now climbs more steeply and eventually passes through a wire and post gate.   1400

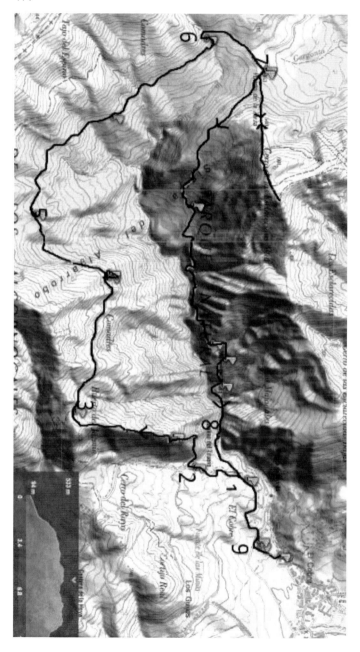

metres from the start of the path, (30 minutes of steep climbing), you meet a track (La Senda de los Prisioneros) where you turn right (MAP 3). Follow this track for 20 minutes passing the unfinished bridge, (puente de los prisioneros), and about 100 metres later, turn right down a footpath off the main track marked by a cairn (MAP 4). Continue along the path, overgrown in places and later quite tricky to follow until you reach the ruins of La Manzanete which comprise just a few stone walls. Here you ignore the first path to the right if you see one, (this is taken from another set of instructions, but we never noticed this path), but take the right fork (MAP 5) at the end of the walls marked by a cairn, heading west, then north-west, roughly following the contour lines between 450 and 500 metres. After 2 kilometres or so (40 minutes), having crossed 3 streams and passed a charcoal oven, following cairns as the path is indistinct in places, you climb up a bank to join a very well-maintained track where you turn right (MAP 6).

Go 600 metres, ignoring one turn to the left and as the track swings hard left turn right on to an open area by some padlocked metal gates (MAP 7). (Gap at the side) (Puerto de la Zarza) If you wish to visit the top of the ridge ahead known as the Cerro de las Escaleretas Altas, take the path going straight ahead and follow it to the top. The views are breath-taking. Return the same way, it is an extra 3 kilometres (1 hour).

Otherwise take a right turn 50 metres from the large gates and pass through a wire and post gate which leads to the path to take you down the side of the valley of the Rio del Miel. It initially climbs a little before descending to join a line of pylons. Pass one turn off to the right which crosses the valley back to the Casa Manzanete. At the next fork you can take either alternative as the two paths meet again after 100 metres or so.

Lower down you take a left fork when there is a bifurcation. After passing through a wire and post gate, you soon reach the ruins of the Molino del Aguila with a couple of defaced panel boards (MAP 8). Turn left to follow the river (right takes you to the mill and a bit further up the river to some waterfalls and places to swim) and then cross a fine pedestrian bridge and then pass by a small flour mill/factory to rejoin the track on which you spent the first part of the walk. Then after 1 kilometre from the factory turn left for the last section (MAP 9).

https://www.wikiloc.com/walking-trails/algeciras-camino-los-prisioneros-return-via-arroyo-del-miel-walk-140-30706009

WALK 142 ALGECIRAS - PUERTO DEL VIENTO - GARGANTA DEL CAPITAN

Time: 4 hours including visits to monuments and tombs (11 Kilometres)

Difficulty: moderate

Terrain: some track but mainly rough paths

BRIEF DESCRIPTION: A walk with an archaeological theme including mills and a tomb, but is also very pretty and full of exciting views and a great swimming spot.

HOW TO GET THERE: from Algeciras take the road from Cobre (CA P 2311) and park 2 kilometres down the road after leaving El Cobre.

THE WALK: from the carpark, follow the track, shortly passing through a gate and after 1 kilometre turn left up a rough track which heads up the hill. (MAP 1) After it curves left then right turn right up a grassier track (MAP 2) which then enters a flatter area heading west. After passing a ruin to your right, the path drops down into a gully and crosses a stream. Immediately the other side, there is a junction of paths. (MAP 3) Turn right and climb out of the valley first heading north then west to arrive at a grassy track where you turn right (MAP 4). Pass a ruin and when you reach a ramshackle farm veer left up into the woods on a rough path marked by an occasional cairn. (MAP 5)

This path climbs in a zigzag fashion for a kilometre eventually following a streambed up a valley to a rather hidden junction of paths. (MAP 6) Turn right, cross the streambed, to climb the side of a ridge for 500 metres passing through a gap (Puerto del Viento) and down into the next valley to very soon meet another junction (MAP 7). Turn right to roughly follow the ridge heading initially east uphill then north, downhill and then east again. The occasional cairn will assist as you descend to a clearing where you turn left to join the SL A 30 the local marked path to the Garganta del Capitan (MAP 8).

Go a short distance and ignore a finger post indicating a path to the right leading to the neolithic tombs some 150 metres down the slope. Keep straight on past a post with a cross on it, to reach the Garganta del Capitan 650 metres further down on the stream of San Pedro (MAP 9). At the stream turn left to continue up to visit the waterfall (swimming spot) at MAP 10 and return downstream on the same path this time keeping straight on to follow the stream downhill. At one point you must turn left where the waypost is hard to see. A few metres down this path there is a sign to the right indicating the Tumba del Capitan. Return to continue downhill to rejoin the stream and then pass Molino San Jose, Molino de las Cuevas. The path leaves the stream and widens to become a track which leads back to the car.

https://www.wikiloc.com/hiking-trails/camino-de-la-trocha-pto-del-viento-garganta-del-capitan-molinos-2019-06-11-37661632

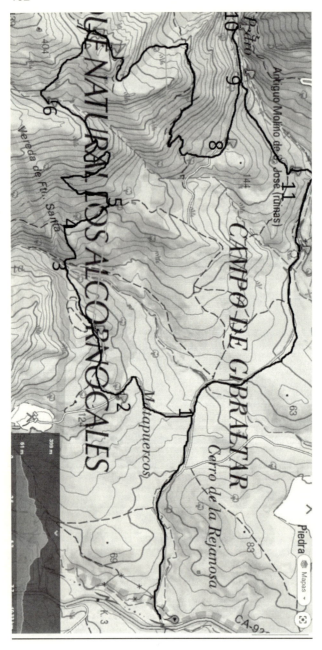

GLOSSARY

Alcalde	mayor
Arroyo	stream
Camino	path, way
Castillo	castle
Cañada	drovers path
Concejal	councillor
Dolmen	burial chamber
Farmacia	chemist
Finca	small farm/ smallholding
Gasolinera	petrol station
Instituto	secondary school
Llano	a flat area / plain
Mirador	viewing point
Rio	river
Senda / sendero	path
Umbria	the shady side of a hill
Venta	a roadside inn
Vereda	path

Made in United States
North Haven, CT
09 January 2024

47232585R00109